p134 violet k

Peaceful Passages

Peaceful Passages

A HOSPICE NURSE'S STORIES OF DYING WELL

JANET WEHR, RN, QTTP

This publication has been generously supported by
The Kern Foundation

QUEST BOOKS

Theosophical Publishing House
Wheaton, Illinois * Chennai, India

First Quest Edition 2015

Quest Books
Theosophical Publishing House
PO Box 270
Wheaton, IL 60187-0270

www.questbooks.com

Cover image: Wylius/Thinkstock
Cover design by Greta Polo
Typesetting by DataPage
Photo credit, text pages: ©iStock.com/etse1112

Library of Congress Cataloging-in-Publication Data

Wehr, Janet.
Peaceful passages: a hospice nurse's stories of dying well / Janet Wehr RN, QTTP—First Quest Edition.
pages cm
Includes index.
ISBN 978-0-8356-0940-1
1. Hospice care. 2. Terminal care. 3. Death. 4. Bereavement. I. Title.
R726.8.W44 2015
616.02'9—dc23 2015006672

Printed in the United States of America

5 4 3 2 1 * 15 16 17 18 19 20

To my dear husband and soul mate, Paul, who always understands and supports the amount of time, energy, love, and grief that it takes for me to do my hospice work. It is you who fills me back up every day, so that I can go out and do it again. My patients and I thank you from the bottom of our grateful hearts. You are my blessing.

I wish you enough sun to keep your attitude bright. I wish you enough rain to appreciate the sun more. I wish you enough happiness to keep your spirit alive. I wish you enough pain so that the smallest joys in life appear much brighter. I wish you enough gain to satisfy wanting. I wish you enough loss to appreciate all you possess. I wish you enough "Hello's" to get you through the final "Goodbye."

—Bob Perks

Contents

Acknowledgments

I wish to acknowledge two experienced and generously willing teachers who helped to shape my hospice career. Both of these gentle but strong women truly "walked the walk," both in their hospice role and in their lives outside that role.

Beverly Spaulding, who had worked as a hospice nurse long before this fledgling nurse came along, took it upon herself to mentor me with all she had gleaned along the way in her practice, much of which had to do, not with book learning, but with the exquisite treasure of her experience. Mary Brooks, hospice social worker extraordinaire (and the best in the land!), taught me the gentle art of when to speak and when to listen and, most importantly, how to make the distinction with one's heart. Mary was also the very first person to read my book manuscript and to coax me persistently to publish it.

To these women, and to countless other people with whom I have walked the hospice path, I thank you for all you have given me.

Namasté.

Introduction

Why Hospice? Or, How the *Peaceful Passages* Book Came to Be

Why hospice? This is the first question I have learned to expect when I'm asked about what kind of nursing I practice. This same question has come from family members, friends, strangers, and nurses and doctors who practice in other areas of the medical field. In most areas of healthcare, saving a life is the focus, and death is often viewed as a failure. Historically, there has not been a great deal of understanding as to why people would choose to concentrate their efforts where a medical success is not likely. Believe me when I say that it required a monumental shift in thinking for me to switch gears from the type of nursing I had previously done, which had everything to do with fixing, saving, and curing. I had to find out for myself that what we do in hospice is every bit as important, except that it's for people who no longer have those treatment options.

"But aren't you sad all the time?" or, "Isn't it scary?" or, "Don't you cry a lot?" are other frequently asked questions. Those of us working in hospice will answer: No, I'm not sad all of the time. No, it isn't scary. Yes, I cry a lot. But the crying is often from the relief, joy, and satisfaction that a patient's last weeks, days, or hours were fulfilling and comfortable, and that their family members had been able to work toward this same goal in a positive way.

Our training to provide symptom management, comfort, and teaching, as well as our ability to foster support and ease in the dying process, has value beyond compare to the patients and families who experience this situation firsthand and often for the first time. In a way, hospice staff can be thought of as midwives during the labor of dying: we are there to teach, support, and guide, without interfering in the process or in the experience that is taking place for patients and their families.

At one point, early in my career, I began to doubt my ability to do this work. I wonde red to myself: What qualifies *me* to assist people through their dying experiences, through what is probably the single most important event in their lives since birth?

During the time that I was wrestling with these questions, I was assigned a patient, Mary Kay, who was exactly my age and who had three children in their early twenties, the same ages as my own children. At times, our lives were so parallel that I felt as if I were looking in a mirror. Mary Kay's children were her primary caregivers during her time in hospice.

One day, as I got out of my car to go into Mary Kay's home for a nursing visit, Mary Kay's neighbor was backing out of her driveway. She stopped her car beside me, rolled down her window, and said, "Are you Janet?" I nodded and saw big tears roll down her cheeks.

"Do you know how much you mean to them?" she asked, pointing to Mary Kay's house. "Do you know that they wait by the windows and the front door for you every day because they rely on your support and expertise so much? Do you know that you do what the rest of us are unable to do because we're afraid? Thank you, Janet."

Well, there was the answer to the question I had been grappling with, in triplicate: we do hospice care because we can, because we're called to do it, and because we make a difference.

I should make the distinction here that the members of the hospice team are really only the people *behind* the scenes. I say this because, with teaching and support, the families and caregivers of our patients actually facilitate the most important parts of care during dying. I've witnessed the tender things family members do to ease a patient's suffering while they guide them toward death with love and compassion; the way they impeccably feed them and keep them clean and comfortable; and the way they nurture the mind, the body, and the spirit of their dying loved one. I've seen them tuck beloved items into their hands, or under their blankets, to bring them joy. I've seen them climb into the patient's hospital bed with them, at their own discomfort, to give them the gift of physical closeness. I've seen them lovingly give a patient their permission to go, bravely telling them that they'll be okay, even as they doubt the words they're saying because their hearts are missing them already. Those of us working in hospice are the facilitators, but the husbands, wives, children, grandchildren and friends are what hospice is all about.

Working in hospice care is an exceptionally diversified area of nursing. We experience exposure to, and understanding of, all cultures and all spiritual backgrounds in the very intimate setting of our patients' homes, and we are often invited to participate in their rituals. Opportunities for observing family members performing daily Reiki treatments on their mother, blessing their father with holy water, chanting Hindu prayers for their sister, or praying in Yiddish for their father has provided me a global education of these practices that I most likely would otherwise never have had the chance to experience in this very personal way.

Despite the fact that we converse with the terminally ill and the dying on a daily basis, there is so much we don't really know about what is happening for these people on this very individual, and in many ways solitary, journey. Sometimes, though, opportunities like the ones described below arise that allow us to glimpse the beauty and the glory that the dying person is experiencing:

- When Alan, one of my patients, was dying, he asked me, "Do you see all of the angels in this room?" Counting out loud, he said, "There are two . . . ten . . . nineteen angels here right now!"
- Ryan told me, "You might think I'm crazy, because my brother died over five years ago, but he was right here last night telling me it's almost time for me to go."

- Jim told me that he clearly dreamed of seeing his parents and brothers, all of whom were deceased, sitting around a table playing poker with one empty chair at the table. This appealed to his sense of humor and highlighted the loneliness he felt for his family, and it gave him great peace in his last days.
- Eva shared that she had had a near-death experience forty years ago and that what she experienced during that event was so *magnificent* that she had vowed never to use that word to describe anything else in her lifetime. She effortlessly coasted toward the moment of death with the peace and conviction of knowing what awaited her, because she had seen it.

These experiences, when they occur, are humbling, sacred, and treasured in the hearts of hospice staff. To know that a patient has transitioned from life to death without pain or anxiety, and with as much love and compassion as possible, is the reward of all hospice workers.

Rather quickly, a strong and personal relationship develops when someone who has previously been a stranger becomes a friend in the intensely emotional situation that their stay in hospice creates. I knew from my very first hospice patient, and her subsequent death, that I would need to find ways to channel that depth of emotion that I felt during and after caring for these patients. Since those first days, I have attended many funerals and memorial services, and I maintain some contact with family members after the death of their loved one. I consider this contact an integral and meaningful part of my work.

That first hospice case, which touched me so deeply, set me on a course of knowing that hospice care was what I was meant to do. As a way of memorializing the patients who began to intensely impact my life and nursing career, I started a journal in which I recorded every name, as well as the date of death, of every patient I cared for. The journal grows with every passing year as I add new names and memories to the pages. In quiet moments, when I open up the journal, I can immediately remember the patients who have passed through my life and given me the honor of caring for them until it was their time to leave the earth. They are the ones who have given ME a gift.

The journal was called *Gone to Heaven* from the first moment I started to record the names in it and evolved into *Peaceful Passages* as the stories wove together. My wish is that the readers of *Peaceful Passages* will not only get a glimpse of the special people who have taught me my hospice "craft" but will also gain new understanding of hospice and the dying process, and the solemn beauty of transitioning from this life.

All the stories in this book are about real people, and all of the events recorded are actual experiences during my nursing career. The question may arise as to whether these are typical hospice experiences or whether I have documented only the miraculous ones. Although the types of experiences I relate may not occur at each and every death, they do occur a great deal of the time, if one is aware. I believe that *every* death is as much a miracle as every birth, whether or not our society allows us to view it that way. We need to look for the miracle in all that happens, whether it appears miraculous or mundane. Albert Einstein said, "there are two ways to live your life: One is as though nothing is a miracle. The other is as though *everything* is."

My main motivation for relating these stories is to encourage people to go into the dying experience knowing and accepting what it *can be* for those who are traveling the journey with the dying. I would like for people to have permission and a reason to go into the encounter with an open mind and an open heart about what is occurring when they are on this holy ground. My hope is that these stories will encourage and enhance a person's opportunity to be knowledgeable about dying and to be ready to witness glory or simply to find themselves in the presence of it.

Readers: If you find it helpful to do so, please feel free to substitute the name of the place that I have termed *heaven* with the *afterlife*, the *hereafter*, or whatever name your belief system employs to describe life after death.

Part One

Understanding Death

When your heart weeps for what it has lost,
your soul laughs for what it has found.

—Sufi Aphorism

Dying is a process unto itself in its cause, length or brevity; reluctance or readiness; intensity or ease. Each of us will have our own individual and specific physical, emotional, and spiritual needs when our time arrives.

The best way we can prepare for our own death and the death of those we care for is not by spending a lifetime trying to hide from it, but rather by embracing death as a natural progression of life.

I'm pleasantly surprised and a bit in awe of patients who talk about their dying as matter-of-factly as they talk about every other part of their lives: "I'd like to read this book, but I'm not sure I'll have time to finish it before I go." "I have one more letter to write to my grandchildren, and then I'll be ready to die." "Why don't we try to go to Florida once more before my time comes?"

Think about it, talk about it, familiarize yourself with it, and read about it as you walk through your life. You just may realize, surprisingly, that the resistance you once felt toward death has disappeared or at least faded to a paler shade of its former intensity.

Chapter 1

The First One

The call came at 2:15 a.m. It was my first on-call summons since I had become a hospice nurse a month earlier. I dressed quickly, running a comb through my sleep-flattened hair, feeling more than a little like firemen do as they jump into their boots and slide down the pole when the alarm sounds. I reviewed the patient's name and address and the message the triage nurse had given me on the phone: "Madeline D. is close to dying. Her family is expecting you as soon as you can get there." On the way, I carefully remembered what I had been taught to do when I arrived. My heart would tell me what to say.

Taking a deep breath, I knocked on the door of the small but cozy apartment. Madeline's granddaughter, Christine, answered, and it was obvious that she had been crying. Christine's husband, Jack, was there to support her. I took a moment to comfort them, then went into the bedroom. Madeline lay in a hospital bed under a pink comforter. She was very old and frail, shrunken to just a wisp of a person. Her knees were drawn up to her chest as if she were going back into the womb. Her fingernails and toenails were a pale shade of blue, the color of the inside of a seashell, showing that her weakened heart could no longer perfuse even this child-sized body. Her breathing was raspy with what is known as the "death rattle," and there were long gaps between breaths. I knew that she was only a few hours, maybe minutes, from dying.

I began gently to discuss with Christine and Jack the physiology of what they were witnessing in Madeline's condition—the signs and symptoms of dying. They listened carefully, relaxed in knowing that what was happening was the normal process of a body letting go of life. Christine related to me that, only two days earlier, Madeline had shared that she was tired, she was old, she had had a rich life, and now she wanted to rest. She had said this calmly, quietly, and with complete satisfaction and conviction in her voice.

Unexpectedly, a man I did not recognize then burst through the door into the apartment. It was apparent that he was angry and wanted to take charge. He was introduced as Christine's brother, Robert, who was a prominent surgeon at our hospital. Robert stormed past us and went into the room where Madeline lay so close to dying. He visually assessed her for no more than a few seconds, then moved briskly to the phone and dialed 911. When he had ordered an ambulance, he turned to me and yelled, "What do you think you're doing? My grandmother is dying! She needs emergency treatment NOW!"

I'm a good "diffuser" in most situations, and I calmly began to explain why this was not an emergency. "Your grandmother is ninety-nine years old," I said. "Her doctor explained to your family that there was no treatment for her age-related illness and decline. She can't see, she can't hear, and now she can't swallow. Perhaps she doesn't want to stay any longer."

Robert simply glared at me, tapping his foot with impatience, waiting for the paramedics to arrive.

And they did. When Robert opened the door to let them in and introduced himself in a loud, authoritative done as "Doctor," all the king's men jumped into action and whisked Madeline out of the house and into the waiting ambulance, leaving Christine, Jack, and me with our mouths hanging open.

What had just happened here? None of the training I had received for working as a hospice nurse had prepared me for this. I felt that I had let Madeline down and prayed that she would not die in a speeding vehicle or in the emergency room amongst strangers. I prayed that the emergency room personnel would not intubate her or perform CPR. I wanted what Jack and Christine wanted, which was for her to be in her own bed, in her own home, with people who loved her and understood her desire to leave. I packed up my nursing bag and left Madeline's home, feeling as if I had failed her.

I was called back to Madeline's home the very next day, to hear from Christine what I already knew: the emergency room staff had taken one look at Madeline the night before and told the "Doctor" that his grandmother wasn't sick, she was dying, and that they felt they should send her back home. Madeline held on until she was back under her fluffy down comforter, in her little pink bedroom, and quietly slipped away.

Chapter 2

Hospice On Call

When the pager goes off, it's 2:00 a.m., and I reluctantly leave my dreams and my soft bed and jump into action. I go to where my clothes have been laid out the night before to save time if a call comes. I dress quickly, barely bothering with my hair, because I am needed somewhere. Someone has died.

I leave home in the dark, following directions from the hospice information sheet. Even though I've been to this home many times in the daylight, I surely don't want to get lost at this hour.

I pull up in front of the house. I center myself for a minute so that I can be the calm in the storm that is probably waiting inside.

A man with a tear-stained face greets me wordlessly at the door and walks me to the back bedroom. Then he disappears around a corner, not wanting me to see him cry.

There, in the hospital bed, is the person who has died. A tiny, attractive grandmother. No heartbeat, no breaths. Pupils fixed and eyes at half-mast. I wonder about who she was, what things she had done during her life, whom she loved, and who loved her.

I tell a young woman, who introduces herself as the patient's daughter, that her mother has died. Two teenaged granddaughters standing at the door burst into tears as they hear the word they expect but have been dreading.

I turn off the oxygen and remove the oxygen tubing from the grandmother's nose. I whisper condolences and tell the family to take as much time as they need. I explain that there are official phone calls that need to be made to the coroner, the doctor, and the funeral home, and I excuse myself to make them while they grieve. I call the doctor to report that his patient has died. The physician has cared for this patient a long time, and I can sense sadness as he asks me to give his condolences.

I call the coroner and the funeral director, both of whom I know now on a first-name basis—these people who work during the wee hours of the morning, just as I do. I tell them the official time of death I pronounced: 2:30 a.m.

I offer to bathe the patient and dress her before the funeral director arrives to take her away. The daughter leaves to gather the necessary items, and I sense her relief at being able to perform one last, loving task for her mother. I bathe the body, tenderly and respectfully, while the rest of the family waits in the next room. This woman has been sick a long time. She is withered and wasted away. She still has blue ink marks on her chest and abdomen where the radiologists aimed the radiation treatments that were meant to help her. I dress her in the clothes provided by her daughter: clean undergarments, a soft blue sweater, black velour pants, cozy socks. I comb through her hair and take a moment to spread lotion on her face so that she will smell good when they kiss her goodbye.

The doorbell rings, and there is a white van in the driveway: the funeral director is here. I encourage the family to say their goodbyes and explain that it might be easier if they wait in the other room while we transfer the body. They decide to stay.

I help the director transfer the woman's body to a gurney and watch as the bag is zipped up over her face. This is always difficult—the finality of it—although I've witnessed it hundreds of times.

I pack up stray medical supplies, strip the bed, and tidy the room. I dispose of medications in the bag of kitty litter that I keep in my nursing bag just for this purpose. I turn off the light and close the door behind me.

The family is grateful for my guidance and support during this difficult time. After my numerous visits over the past several weeks, they say they will never forget me. Despite the fact that I will repeat this scenario over and over again, little do they realize that they and their loved one are likewise etched in my heart forever. My watch says 4:00 a.m. I leave the home, get into my car, and turn the key. The pager goes off.

Someone has died.

Chapter 3

For Comfort's Sake

Not surprisingly, laypersons who are caring for ill family members at home often presume that the medications that are used at the end of life *cause* death. The prevailing reason for this belief is that very sick people often *do* die while using these medications. But it is of utmost importance to clarify that the real cause of death for such people is the disease process itself, not the medications that promote comfort at the end of life. Morphine is one of these medications, and it is given routinely in hospitals, in other clinical settings, and at home, with no concern whatsoever to causing death. It is the same in hospice care, and I'll say it again: *comfort medications don't cause death; illnesses cause death.*

A few years ago, Ada, a woman who was of a religious faith that did not allow its members to seek medical help or to take medications, was added to my caseload of patients.

Ada's husband, Charlie, had made the initial contact with hospice, and I met with him before I met with Ada. Within minutes of introducing myself, I saw him crumble into a heap of despair while he told me his wife's story. Ada was sixty-three years old and had end-stage breast cancer.

Because of her religious beliefs, she had not seen a physician for this or any previous health conditions, nor had she taken any medication to help with pain. Months ago, she had closed herself off in an upstairs bedroom, and since then she had rarely seen visitors except for Charlie. The reason was this: her left breast was being devoured by the cancer that was growing there, and the smell was horrific. She isolated herself from other people, including her children, so as not to embarrass herself or offend others with this problem. This was bad enough, Charlie cried, but his wife was in so much pain that he just couldn't stand to watch her suffer anymore. He told me tearfully but with conviction that he was ready to break his vow to his church for both him and Ada and wanted to begin giving Ada medication to ease her pain.

I empathized with Charlie, but I knew that if Ada was of sound mind and able to make her own decisions, it would be she who had to make this choice.

When I got to the upstairs room where Ada had chosen to hide herself, I found something that made my heart break, and it wasn't the smell that I found so overwhelming it made me feel dizzy. Ada was sitting in a chair, hunched over a small table, with her upper body balanced on her elbows, which was the one and only position she found she could tolerate due to the severity of her pain. Charlie, who had followed me upstairs to his wife's room, told me that at night he put a pillow down on the table so that she could rest her head. He said that she had been unable to lie down or sit back in the chair for weeks. Every movement, every breath, every attempt at sleep was an ordeal of pain.

I began to tell Ada that there were things I could do to help her. When I told her I could get a hospital bed that we could adjust for her comfort, she stared. When I told her that I could get dressings to eliminate the odor of her cancer, I had her full attention. When I told her I wouldn't rest until I knew *she* could rest, she started to weep. "All I want is to be able to lie in a soft bed. All I want is to take a breath and not have it hurt. All I want to do is to go to sleep."

Charlie moved closer to his wife then and told her in a quiet voice that he had changed his mind about a few things, and one of them was their religious conviction not to take medications that could help them. "You aren't against science, are you?" he asked gently. "God gave us science, and science made these things available. Maybe we've been ungrateful not to use what God has provided." Ada didn't have to think about it very long. She nodded silently at Charlie, then whispered to me, "I'll do whatever will help me." "Thank you, God. Thank you, Charlie," I prayed silently.

It is a well-known fact among hospice nurses that pain or anxiety can keep a patient in a lingering pattern during their dying. A person can become so focused on the physical feelings they are experiencing with their body that they can't relax enough to let go and allow death to occur. My belief is that when medications are given and interventions are performed to promote comfort and relaxation, the mind and the heart of a person can enter into the necessary quiet place that will allow them to connect with their spirit. It's as if the physical body can finally exhale and say to the soul, "I'm done. You take over for me now."

Within two hours, a hospital bed was set up in Ada's room with the best, softest mattress that was available. Medications for pain, anxiety, and the other end-of-life symptoms were on the dresser with instructions for their use. I cleaned and dressed Ada's left breast wound with a dressing that contained a charcoal filter to eliminate odor. I asked her if she would take a dose of pain medication before we attempted to transfer her to the new bed, and she agreed.

After waiting fifteen minutes for Ada to relax and for the medication to take effect, Charlie and I lifted her delicate, little body out of the chair she had sat in for so long and laid her gently on the bed. We covered her with a soft, yellow flannel sheet and stood back. It was the first time in several weeks that Ada had been able to lie down and rest her sick body. She sank into the bed's softness, and I heard her sigh. Although her eyes were closed, her face broke into a sweet, heavenly smile, and she said almost inaudibly, "Now I have everything I want."

Once Ada was comfortable, she never spoke or moved a muscle all night. She died just before sunrise the next morning, having found the peaceful place she needed so that her spirit could soar and she could leave her body behind.

Chapter 4

Not Yet

As hospice workers, we are well aware that hearing is the last of the senses to shut down during the dying process, and there is growing evidence that patients can hear right up until the time that death claims them. They often lack the energy or the focus to converse in the way they used to, but they continue to be aware of who is present and other small details of daily life. We urge family members and friends to talk to their loved one and especially to share what is in their hearts, even though the patient appears to be nonresponsive or in a comatose state. We know that the time dying persons spend in apparent sleep is time they are actually processing what they need to do to accomplish passing from this world. It isn't unusual for a patient who hasn't verbally responded or been alert in many days suddenly to contribute a comment to a conversation going on around them or to rouse, if only briefly, to make a statement, ask a question, or connect in some other, important way. We teach families to talk to the dying person and to share information with them, such as the day, the date, and plans for who might be visiting. Even if the person seems to be unaware of what is going on in their environment, we encourage their families to talk to them as if they were listening, because they are. If doing so can contribute to a peaceful passing, it is well worth the effort, even though the family might feel it's in vain at times.

Sometimes the dying person is waiting for one more element of closure to conclude their business before making their final passage. One male patient survived several days longer than the expected seven to fourteen days for someone in a comatose state who had thus not received food or fluids during that time. The body's organs suffer from dehydration after only a few days; yet this man was almost sixteen days into the process, and we did not see any of the obvious changes associated with imminent death. I understood the reason after I spoke to his wife. She told me that their son lived in China and that the only flight he had been able to book would not arrive for another twenty-four hours. She had held the phone up to her husband's ear so that their son could reassure his dad. "I'm coming, Dad. I love you. I'll be there on Friday at 8:00 p.m." Sure enough, our patient was still lingering on Friday at 8:00 p.m. He had the closure with his son that he had waited for and died at 9:00 p.m., having checked the final item off his "to do" list before he left.

Chapter 5

Dying with Dignity

I become happy when I think about Sarah. Sarah was everything I'd like to be: beautiful, funny, practical, smart, brave, well-educated, and dignified. It was the dignified part that I love the most. Her dignity was a combination of integrity, decisiveness, and determination, and it was evident in every aspect of the way she lived her life.

The first time I called to make an appointment with Sarah for a nursing visit, it occurred to me that I wasn't fitting her into *my* schedule, *she* was fitting me into *hers*! "No," she said, "Monday won't work because I'm going to the theater and out to lunch with some friends. Tuesday . . . nope. I have exercise class. Maybe Wednesday. No, I'm going shopping that day. Okay, Thursday is open. But only in the morning." I looked down at the information sheet I had been given regarding Sarah and her health history. Could this woman really have both colon cancer and pulmonary fibrosis? She sounded busier than I was!

When I arrived at Sarah's house on Thursday, I waited outside the front door while she herded her two little dogs into a bedroom. One of her dogs, Baxter, a little three-legged terrier, was skittish around strangers. Although the other one was small, she referred to him as "a beast," so I didn't particularly want to meet him, anyway. They were Sarah's constant companions, and she began planning for their care early in her illness so that she would have a say in their destiny after she was gone.

Sarah put the "D" word on the table as soon as I sat down. "Now, I know I'm dying, but I'm really busy doing the things I like before I can't manage to do them anymore, so I think you only need to come twice a month." Sarah was only sixty-nine years old, but she looked much younger. She was stylish in an understated way and always beautifully groomed and well-dressed. The only thing marring the perfect picture was the oxygen tube running from her nose, across the floor, and over to the concentrator, making its soft whirring sound in the corner. Prior to being diagnosed with colon cancer, Sarah had been diagnosed with pulmonary fibrosis, a serious condition in which the lungs lose their elasticity, making breathing difficult, even at rest. Sarah had lost her husband to cancer four years earlier, and she had received both of these diagnoses just a short time later. Knowing this about Sarah made me wonder where she got her stamina to go on.

Sometimes when patients are this matter-of-fact about their dying, I wonder if they are in some denial about the reality of their condition, but this was not the case with Sarah. She explained that she had gone through the stages of anger, denial, bargaining, sadness, "and a few others" and had found her way to acceptance at long last. She had made a "to-do" list that included getting in touch with people she hadn't seen in a while and writing personal letters to all her grandchildren. She was *so* ready to go, she said, that her grown children—her daughter, Amy, and her son, Angelo—were taking offense at her apparent eagerness to "be done with it." Sarah had strong spiritual beliefs resulting from her years of education in theology. She had helped her husband to die peacefully at the end of his illness, and she had no fear of the dying process or of what might come after. She did, however, feel strongly about preparing those around her in every way that she could.

After several months, Sarah began to feel the toll that her cancer was taking on her body, and she was forced to slow down her activity. She took the time to set up several meetings with hospice staff when her son and daughter could be present to ask questions. In her forthright manner, Sarah would lead the discussion, asking the questions she felt needed answers. "Okay, now tell us what happens right after I die, who they have to call, and how to tell if I'm really dead." Sarah's greatest concern, she told me on more than one occasion, was that no one would be there to help her children at the moment of her death. She felt strongly that they should not be alone at that time.

Sarah was prepared for many months and prepared everyone around her, right down to the letter. However, she seemed to have come to a stalemate in her dying process, and she was not happy about it. Sarah's son, Angelo, would come to visit her at the home of her daughter, Amy, where she went to live when she became too weak to be on her own. Angelo would arrive for a visit, glance in Sarah's direction, and tease, "Oh. Are you still around?" Sarah would frown.

As Sarah lost more ground physically, she succumbed to weakness and the need to be dependent on her daughter for her personal care and most of her needs. Amy embraced the role of caregiver as no one else I have ever seen in her competency, her patience, and her willingness to be of service to her mother. As she performed the daily care routines of personal hygiene and medication administration, she developed a very keen nursing intuition that I believe surprised even her. As much as most patients struggle against the need to be dependent on others, Sarah took it all in stride. There was none of the usual embarrassment about nakedness or having personal cares performed by someone else, or of relying on others for simple tasks. Sarah would shrug and say, "It is what it is." On one tragic occasion, when Sarah fell to the floor attempting to get out of bed, her only reaction was one of disappointment that she didn't get a "shiner" to show for her trouble, although she did frequently hold up a mirror to admire a small bruise that appeared on her cheek several days later!

Oh, Sarah and all her family members were prepared for Sarah to die. But nothing happened. She had already outlived her prognosis by more than a year; she was tired of living in a sick body, and she was ready to leave it behind. She told me during one visit that she wanted to hurry the process along. Of course, I was quick to explain that hospice would not, could not, hasten her death. I added, though, that people do sometimes make the choice to stop eating and drinking entirely in order to bring a more rapid end to their life, and that this is more difficult than it sounds. Sarah asked me how long it would take to die if she did this.

I told her twelve days was the average, but it could be slightly shorter or longer. Sarah didn't stop to think about it. She decided right then and there, as she pushed away the glass of water she had been given by Amy, that to stop drinking and eating was what she would do.

Up to that point in my career as a hospice nurse, I had known only a handful of patients who had consciously chosen to take this route; and, of those few, none had succeeded. It takes a great deal of stamina and determination to resist food and fluids. The spirit is usually willing but the body is weak, for when a hungry person smells food, or a thirsty mouth feels parched, resolve dissipates quickly. However, true to Sarah's strong nature and her desire to return home, she persisted.

Amazingly, the human body compensates for lack of hydration and nutrition in an interesting way. Anyone who has ever been on a diet knows that the first three days are the most difficult. After that, the body produces endorphins that not only eliminate hunger pangs but also provide a feeling of well-being and euphoria that allows the person to feel very light and emotionally calm and content. This is what happened for Sarah after the first seventy-two hours, and then she began the dying process that she so longed for.

On the eighth day of Sarah's fast, she was in a coma and showing signs of imminently dying. I had seen her the day before and hadn't expected her to live through the night. However, she was still breathing when I arrived the next morning at Amy's home along with Shannon, the nursing assistant who had come to bathe her. Knowing how classy and particular Sarah had always been about her appearance, Amy, Shannon, and I decided to bathe, groom, and dress her for her final journey. Angelo, always the entertainer, kept up a running stream of funny, sentimental stories about Sarah from the other side of the privacy screen while we gently went about our task.

Only minutes after we finished bathing her, rubbing lotion on her skin, combing her hair, and dressing her in her favorite nightgown, Sarah's condition began to change drastically. Her breathing became increasingly shallow, with longer periods between. Her color became very pale; her hands and feet became cold. With Angelo and Amy on each side holding her hands, and Shannon and me at the foot of the bed, we all sent silent, loving energy to Sarah and said our final goodbyes as she slipped away to the place she had longed for. It was like watching a little candle go out, a flame growing smaller and smaller and then quietly extinguishing.

Sarah taught us nothing about fear. Or sadness. Or regrets. Or bitterness. No; in her gentle and persistent way, Sarah taught us about dying with dignity.

Postscript: When Sarah moved to Amy's house toward the end of her illness, she decided that "the Beast" should be put to sleep because, with his ornery personality, he would not settle in with another family. Her little three-legged Baxter she gave to her cousin, who lived an hour away. Her cousin reported to Amy and Angelo that, at the moment of Sarah's death, Baxter began crying and howling, sensing, even from that great distance, that his special master was gone.

Chapter 6

"I'm Coming, Dad"

George had been actively dying for a couple of days. In "active dying," a person experiences multiple changes in his physicality that are obvious and expected to professionals trained in end-of-life care or to people who have witnessed the dying process before. Certainly, in a small percentage of deaths the patient just goes to sleep, never to awaken. Most of us feel that when this occurs it is a true gift because it happens with such ease. But more often, there is a set pattern of stages in the dying process that help those around the dying person prepare for the coming event. There is a "labor" to dying, some work that needs to be done for letting go, just as there is a labor to grabbing hold of life during birth. Again, this is the reason that hospice workers arc called "midwives of the soul." Like labor in birthing, there is often a stopping and a starting, a pulling and a pushing, an opening and a closing of the process at hand. Some, but not all, of the symptoms are universal, and what may take one person weeks or months to experience, another may pass through in just hours.

Most common, and most noticeable to a witness, is the distancing of the dying person from previous activities, interests, and even people. The attention is turned from the outside world to the inside world, where significant changes are taking place in preparation for death. This also includes a lack of interest in eating or drinking, which is likely the "wisdom of the body" dictating that these things are no longer needed and indeed may make the process more difficult if continued. Sleeping, or simply resting with the eyes closed, is done most of the day and night-time hours. Patients who are able to explain this behavior say that it is due to a combination of spending time doing personal "life review," letting go, and preparing for the dying experience itself. As weakness overcomes strength, things such as continence of bodily waste, the ability to swallow, and the energy to rouse oneself to speak diminishes greatly or disappears altogether. Vital signs fluctuate as the body struggles to regain a balance that it can no longer find, finally settling on a decreasing blood pressure and an elevated pulse. Color and temperature changes, particularly to hands and feet, can go from warm to cold or pink to dusky and back again for many hours. The lungs struggle to find a rate and pattern that can conserve energy; the initial shallow, slow breathing can change to rapid panting or periods of apnea (gaps between breaths) as the body loses more ground in its efforts.

I can't stress enough that even during these erratic times, it is important to remember that the dying person's hearing is intact. I urge everyone who is caring for someone during their dying experience to remember this and use it to promote comfort and closure.

George was nearing the finish line in his dying process; all of the expected signs and symptoms had occurred over several weeks, several days, and, most significantly, in the past several hours. We knew that his body would not be able to function much longer.

I had just entered George's room in the nursing home, along with Theresa, one of the nurses who worked there. All of the signs of dying were present, including apnea, which means that his condition was progressing toward certain death. Theresa and I were repositioning George in his bed and straightening his linens to keep him comfortable. As we gently turned him onto his back, it became obvious that his breathing had ceased altogether. For the next full minute, I attempted to find a pulse, but none was present. At this very moment, a second nurse, Laura, entered the room. Before we could inform her that George had passed away, she announced loud enough for George to hear, "I just saw George's wife, Louise, coming down the hall. And her son called to say he would be here by 5:30."

Miraculously, and very unexpectedly, George, who was still unconscious, twitched and began to breathe. Louise was able to visit her husband at his bedside until their son arrived at the time he was expected. George passed away at 7:30 p.m. with his family present. George, it appears, chose to come back to make certain that he, his wife, and his son all had the closure they needed.

Chapter 7

One Last Wish

A pattern that hospice workers notice many times is that a large number of patients have a goal, a milestone, that they wish to reach before they succumb to their passing. For example, to one person it may be important to have one more Christmas with their loved ones or to perform a favorite activity one last time. For another, it may be to find the courage to do something they have never done before. For others, it is being able to be present for an anniversary of their wedding, or for the birthday of a family member. When the death occurs on another family member's birthday, I try to get that person to understand that this is a gift; it is likely that mom or dad picked that particular day because it was a day that was already special to them.

The only way to describe William was that he was a crusty old bachelor. He had lived alone for most of his seventy-four years and was not used to taking suggestions—or, in his words, "orders"—from ANYBODY. When he was diagnosed with liver cancer, he refused all treatment for his disease and did his best to alienate the very staff of medical personnel who were trying to help him. In his cantankerous way, and despite my protestations, he insisted that he didn't care whether or not he lived and was just as insistent that "probably no one else cared, either." I would be pleased if I got to the end of the nursing visit without a scowl or a snarl from William, which seems a pitiful goal, but it was a victory, nonetheless.

The one subject that would bring a sparkle to his eye and a gentleness to his voice was fishing. He had been an avid fisherman since he was a child and had continued this solitary sport until he had gotten sick. "Just one more fishing trip" he'd say, "and then I don't care if I live or die." This was going to be easier said than done since William was already weak and wasted away, and he had had several falls while just trying to maneuver around his tiny little house.

William had three brothers from whom he had become estranged over the years. I had William's permission to discuss his medical condition and prognosis with one of them, whom he had named as his power of attorney for healthcare. I told the brother about William's wish for one last fishing trip. To William's surprise, the three brothers chose a place and a date, then called William and invited him to go on a fishing trip with them. Although William continued to decline, he spent the next few weeks repairing his lures, packing his tackle box, and actually SMILING! I made a thorough list of the essential items that William would need on the trip, including medications, wheelchair, and diapers for his recent incontinence issues. I had also given his brothers the name and phone number of a hospice in the area where they planned to stay, "just in case."

I explained the kinds of help that William would need with his personal care because he was so weak, and I prefilled a medication box. His brothers listened attentively, wanting to ensure a safe and enjoyable trip for William. Two days before the scheduled outing, I felt comfortable that all the details had been covered.

The big day came, and William's brothers arrived at the crack of dawn to pick him up. All his fishing equipment was packed and ready at the front door, but William wasn't there, waiting; William had died during the night. I thought then, and still do, that just the idea of one last fishing trip with his three brothers had brought the closure William needed in order to let go. I wondered, too, if he wasn't promised better fishing on the "other side" of the lake.

Chapter 8

Hospice 101

One of the first criteria I set for my initial visit with a patient and family who have entered the hospice program is to make sure they have no questions about the hospice philosophy or what our mission and purpose is in regard to the care we provide for our patients. It is really incredible to me how far from actuality their understanding can sometimes be, and it is important to make sure that there are no misunderstandings. I often hear people say, "Hospice helps you die." We don't, actually, and I gently correct them by saying, "Hospice doesn't help you die. Hospice helps you *live* until you die," because hospice is all about bringing quality to life, not hastening death.

It is also important to outline the Medicare or insurance benefits to hospice patients as to what specific services are being made available to them, because it allows them to let go of many of the details that tend to bog them down during this already difficult and trying time. A large medical bill could be incurred, for example, by a hospice patient who decides to be admitted to the hospital for more aggressive treatment of their disease without first having revoked their hospice benefit. A patient is always able to choose to revoke their hospice care if that is their decision, with no questions asked, allowing themselves once more to be eligible for curative or experimental treatment. However, it is critical to remember, in that situation, that there is a protocol to follow that is important and necessary to stay within legal boundaries.

I had just finished explaining this to a new hospice family, as well as having read them the patient's-rights form and the Privacy Act. They were nodding their heads in complete agreement and smiling throughout the explanation. Billy, the patient, had been sick with COPD, a lung disease, for many years, and he and his family could see that his quality of life now was almost nonexistent. He wanted to die, and they wanted to see him out of his miserable condition of being bedridden and experiencing the anxiety of "air hunger" from his disease.

When I felt I had thoroughly explained what the family needed to know about hospice care and the guidelines, I asked if there were any questions. As Billy's children waited for an answer, one daughter spoke. "So," she said, "we choose the day and time, and then you come and help him die, right?" With great surprise, despite my thorough explanation, I realized she was talking about assisted suicide. Oh, boy. Back to the drawing board.

Another of our nurses had been seeing her patient, Peter, for several weeks. Although his family reported that he did not appear depressed or anxious, the nurse found something very different when she arrived for her visits. During the physical assessment, and during her attempts to converse with him, Peter would refuse to make eye contact. He would answer with a simple yes or no, never sharing his feelings or elaborating with an answer or actual conversation. He appeared physically to fold in on himself at these times and completely shut himself off from communicating. Was this simply Peter's personality? It was not, according to his family.

Our staff always attempts to meet patients where they are in their disease process, in terms both of their understanding and of their level of acceptance of it. There are people who meet their illness head on, people who never reach acceptance of their terminal diagnosis, and people everywhere in between.

Additionally, we always attempt to accept who our patients are as people. Those who have been "loners" all their lives won't be any less so during their dying, and those who have been calm and analytical will probably remain that way until their dying breath. "We die the way we live" is a common hospice saying; and, more often than not, it holds true. We don't change who we are during dying; in fact, we become more authentically who we have been throughout our life.

Because Peter's family described him as outgoing and friendly, the nurse felt strongly that there must be something else that was keeping Peter from relaxing in her presence.

On her fourth visit, the nurse sat down and said, "Peter. At every visit we've had, you seem angry at me and even fearful. I want to help you but I can't if you don't converse with me a little. Is there something I'm doing that makes you respond that way?"

After a long silence, Peter looked directly at her and he said, "It's because I don't know which day you're going to do it."

Confused, the nurse replied, "Do what, Peter?"

As he started to weep, he said, "I don't know which day you're going to give me the pill." The nurse, still confused, was trying to make sense of what Peter was saying, and then it dawned on her. Peter's understanding of hospice was that, on any given visit, the nurse would come and administer a medication that would end his life.

Very gently, and very clearly, the nurse explained that this would never, ever be done, and she began to reeducate Peter on the actual care that hospice would provide. Peter opened up and, from that visit on, was the same friendly guy that his family and friends knew and loved. These misunderstandings taught me to never assume anything and to always assess the perceptions of others along the way on the hospice journey.

Chapter 9

A Water Bug's Tale

This story makes a wonderful analogy of death and dying, and it is often read at funerals or told to young children to help them understand death in a picturesque and sensible way. The source of it is unknown; here's my paraphrased version:

Once upon a time, down below the depths of a pond, there lived a water bug. Not just one water bug, but many. This was their element, and they were very content in the pond. There were plants to eat and to hide behind, rocks to swim around, and rain from above to freshen the water they lived in. If they looked up at the surface of the pond from down below, they could see, at most times, that there was light shining through. Being water bugs, they needed to breathe underwater, but as they swam closer to the surface, they experienced that it felt warm and comfortable. The shimmering of the water's surface made it difficult to see clearly above, but sometimes they could make out the movement of things high above the water, swaying in the breeze or soaring through the air.

One day, one of the water bugs became curious and began to climb the stalk of the reed that he was resting on.

He climbed higher and higher until, all of a sudden, he broke through the surface of the pond. Although he was exhausted, he continued to climb to the very top of the reed. When he could feel the warm sun on his back, he fell asleep, and he stayed asleep for three days.

When the water bug awoke, he was completely refreshed and began to look around. It was beautiful up here! There were trees of all kinds and flowers of all colors! The sky was brilliant blue, and the sun shone like a golden disk in the sky. He saw birds and insects of all sizes and shapes flying in the air, performing dips and dives and swoops. As he looked over his shoulder, he noticed that he was different now. His body had grown longer and he had two beautiful sets of emerald green wings on his back. He was a dragonfly! He began to beat his wings to dry them, and before long, he was soaring through the air with the other creatures.

After a while, he came to rest back on the reed that had allowed him to break through the surface of the water, and he remembered his family and his friends and his life at the bottom of the pond. He missed them, and he wished he could tell them all about his journey and his new life above the water. He knew that he was different now, no longer a water bug but a dragonfly, and that he and his family and friends no longer spoke the same language.

For just a moment, he was sad, but then he looked up at the sky and the new world that awaited him, and he began to fly. He knew that, in turn, each water bug would have the chance to make this same wonderful discovery for itself.

Part Two

Ways of Saying Goodbye

What a friend we have in time, Gives us children, makes us wine.
Tells us what to take or leave behind.

—John Denver

We say it many times every day: "So long"; "Goodbye"; "I'll miss you." But it is never more heartfelt, difficult, or permanent than when we have to find the words at the end of someone's life. When we realize the void that a person's absence will leave in our own life, finding those words becomes harder, but it is needed and even longed for by the one who is leaving.

We are all moving toward the moment of our death from the time we are born. We know that, in the end, none of us escapes death. As children, we expect to lose our parents someday, and married couples contemplate, from time to time, who will be left behind when the other one goes.

The process of finding a way to express this final farewell in a way that is satisfying and comfortable for both parties is as individual as a fingerprint and as necessary as the air we breathe. One need look no further than one's own heart to find the best way to provide this moment of closure.

Sometimes, for a variety of reasons, the letting go doesn't happen until after the death. A friend told me of the heartbreak he felt at losing his father . . . until a rainbow appeared in the sky on the day that he planted a tree in his father's honor. A patient's wife confided that the grief she felt over losing her spouse was nonstop . . . until a letter from him, which had been lost in the mail for two years, arrived in her mailbox after his death. Jeremy, another friend, saw a cardinal on his windowsill moments after his mother died. Now, every time a cardinal appears unexpectedly, he feels that love-connection to his mother.

These people, and many others like them, have found meaningful and unusual ways of letting go of someone dear to them who didn't choose to leave but needed to because death had come. The next selection of stories exemplifies some of the ways these closures have occurred.

Chapter 10

A Baby Angel

None of us want to leave our children or our grandchildren, especially if they are very young. We often fear that they won't remember us or that their tender young hearts will feel the pain of separation from us. We wonder who will take our place in their hearts when we are gone, wanting someone to love them the way we do, yet dreading that we will be replaced.

Our hospice team works hard with the children who have any relationship to the patients we serve. Our social worker guides the type of help that is needed in each situation, and the rest of the team—the nurse, the nursing assistant, the chaplain, and sometimes a volunteer—also helps to bring the children to a place of comfort with the dying process and the death, when it eventually occurs. The hospice bereavement coordinator is ready and waiting in the wings to take over in any way that might be needed to support the family, and especially the children, after the death occurs. There are also excellent resources in bookstores, written in simple language, that introduce children of all ages to the concept of impermanence and death in a way from which they can learn and benefit. The more patients see and sense that the children of the family are prepared, the more they relax and enjoy their final days and weeks.

Children can be encouraged to contribute in any way they feel comfortable in the care of the patient, no matter what the relationship is: parent, grandparent, or family friend. Since many young children are uncomfortable with illness, their own level of comfort may simply allow them to draw or paint pictures that can be given to the person who is dying. Although some children have no qualms about climbing into bed to watch TV with daddy, who is sick, others may hold back and want to blow kisses from the doorway, or write "X's" and "O's" in notes. All children should be praised for whatever steps they can take, however small, in preparation for the death of someone close to them. It will set the stage and give confidence for every time in the future that, inevitably, they will encounter death as they go through their lives.

Jenny's parents first got the news that she had multiple birth defects when her mother was only six months pregnant: Trisomy 18. They read that babies with this defect had anencephaly or microcephaly, meaning that the brain was missing or underdeveloped. These babies usually had extra digits on their hands and feet; were blind and often deaf; had heart deformities; and very often had sutures, meaning the connecting lines of the skull, that were not fused. Doctors told Jenny's parents that it was likely the pregnancy would not go full term and that they could exercise the choice to terminate the pregnancy. In any case, the baby probably would not make it through the birth process.

Jenny's parents were not new to parenting. They had two other daughters, ages two and four. They felt strongly that if they had been given a child with these difficulties, it was because God knew that they could handle it, and they proceeded ahead, as they had with the pregnancies of their other two children, but with several exceptions.

Jenny's parents-to-be found a minister who agreed to be on call in the delivery room, no matter what day or hour the birth occurred. If Jenny wasn't going to make it through the birth, her parents nevertheless wanted a minister present to bless her and baptize her as she was entering the world. They also explained to Jenny's older sisters, in language they could understand, that the new baby would come but she wouldn't be able to stay; that God wanted her in heaven with him where he could take care of her. They were told that, although he loved them just as much, he needed them to stay and show love to their parents and to the world until he called them to be with him and to see Jenny again. By the time the ninth month of the pregnancy arrived, it wasn't uncommon to hear the two little girls discussing Jenny in terms of "after Jenny goes back to heaven," or, "We're just borrowing Jenny, then we have to give her back." I could see how natural the transition would be for these little girls after Jenny died because they already had been told that she wouldn't be able to stay.

Of course, it was a much more difficult task for the parents. Even though they were well aware that the condition Jenny had would be incompatible with life once she was no longer living inside her mother's body, their hearts were broken. They steeled themselves for whatever form her birth would take and prepared themselves as well as they could.

Jenny, it turned out, was a full-term baby. At nine months, almost to the day, her parents went to the delivery room along with the minister whom they had "reserved." Although the predictions regarding the seriousness of Jenny's defects had been accurate, she had made it through the pregnancy, she made it through the birth and the emergency baptism in the delivery room, and she made it through the three-day hospital stay in the special-care nursery. No one had prepared Jenny's parents for taking her home, because the medical experts didn't believe that it would happen, but that's what they did.

I had my first hospice visit at Jenny's home the day she arrived there. It was obvious, when I looked at her, that many genetic defects were present. Her head was too small, flattened on top where her tiny brain hadn't grown to fill the space. Her skull had to be protected when she was lifted or carried, because it seemed to be made up of a number of loose puzzle pieces that didn't quite fit together. The holes for her eyes were very small, and the tiny eyes inside them didn't move or track. She didn't respond to the noises around her, so it appeared that she was deaf. There were extra fingers on each hand and extra toes on each foot. And, in her own unique and mishappened way, she was beautiful. Each time I held her while her parents tried to get a few precious moments of rest, I could feel the special grace from this tiny child of God.

As much as they wanted to spend time with their new baby girl before she died, it was an exhausting struggle for Jenny's parents that she lived almost two weeks. They rarely slept and held her constantly, knowing that, because her little life was so precarious, she might leave them at any moment. She did so quietly, in the middle of the night, lying between her parents in their bed.

This little baby angel came for only a brief moment in time, but in that short span, she taught a lifetime's worth of love, acceptance, and letting go to all who were blessed to have been part of her story.

Chapter 11

Gone from My Sight

I am standing upon a seashore. A ship at my side spreads her white sails to the morning breeze and starts for the blue ocean. She is an object of beauty and strength. I stand and watch her until at length she hangs like a speck of white cloud just where the sea and the sky come to mingle with each other.

Then someone at my side says, "There! She is gone!"

"Gone where?" I ask.

Merely gone from my sight, comes the answer. The ship itself still exists. She is just as large in mast and hull and spar as she was when she left my side, and she is just as able to bear her load of living freight to her destined port.

She is diminished in size merely from my perspective, not in herself. And just at the moment when someone at my side says, "There! She is gone!" other eyes are watching her approach, and other voices are ready to take up the glad shout, "Here she comes!"

And that is dying.

—Anonymous

Chapter 12

The Look of Love

Louie was ninety-four years old and had been a long-time hospice patient. His wife, Lesley, had died in hospice two years earlier, and I had been her nurse at that time, so Louie and his four children were very familiar to me.

Louie was failing, but except for his old age, there didn't seem to be a disease process that could be identified. He simply became weaker and less interested in all the things that he had previously loved. Every time he would start to spiral down into a decline that seemed like it might be his last one, he would suddenly rebound, shocking his family, his caregiver of eight years, and our hospice staff. This pattern recurred again and again during a period of eighteen months. On one visit, he would be unresponsive and appear close to dying; on the next visit he would open his twinkling eyes and say, "Oh! Hi, Doctor!" which was what he always called me during the time I knew him.

Eventually, Louie did have his final decline. Only his son, Lonny, lived in the area. Sons Lloyd and Lance and daughter, Lauren, all lived out of state. They had all made emergency visits to Louie's bedside many other times when they thought he might be dying, so they were skeptical as to whether this was the real event. I'm sure it felt like the story "The Boy Who Cried Wolf" to them, but they each made the trip once again to be sure they had the chance to say goodbye, just in case it was the last time they would see their father.

Louie lay in a coma for several days. He had had no nutrition or hydration, nor had he opened his eyes or spoken for that period of time. He had been turned, bathed, dressed, changed, and cared for, but there hadn't been a single piece of evidence that he was still consciously aware of his environment. On Tuesday, however, he opened his eyes and smiled, holding his finger up to his lips. "Shhhh! Can you hear that?" he said, "That's God talking!" I wish I could say that I heard something, but I didn't. I did, however, call his children into the room to see their father awake. Was this another false alarm? Everything in me said, no, it's not, so I waited.

Louie looked around the room. Then he motioned with his hand for Lonny to approach the bed. Lonny moved forward and took his father's hand. Louie held Lonny's hand for a full five minutes, not breaking eye contact, not saying a word, smiling and nodding slightly. Then he said, "Thank you."

Louie looked past me and said in his weak, quivery voice, "Now I need that one," and pointed at Lauren. Louie took her hand and went through the same process of looking intently at her, as if to memorize every detail, nodding, smiling, and again saying, "Thank you" before he let go of her hand.

Louie did the same with Lloyd and then with Lance. When he had finished, he turned his head to smile at me, said "Okay," closed his eyes, and never opened them again.

Chapter 13

A Sky Full of Crows

I have to admit that initially my heart resisted adding Rob to my caseload of patients for a number of reasons.

First of all, he was fairly young and a new grandparent, and I felt that the similarities of where we were in our lives would be difficult for me to set aside in order to be a good fit as his nurse.

Second, his case was complicated, with numerous attempts having been made by the specialists at the hospital's pain clinic to control the intractable pain of his pancreatic cancer.

Third, his female physician was notoriously difficult to work with, and I knew that we would be interfacing often in view of the complexity of Rob's disease process. There was also the potential for Rob to need abdominal drains, IVs, and nerve blocks to manage his symptoms of discomfort. Moreover, the nurse who admitted Rob to hospice care had alluded to the fact that his family was not "on board" with Rob's diagnosis or with the prognosis that he didn't have much time. Rob's parents still hadn't directly addressed their knowledge of Rob's disease to him; instead, it sat like an elephant in the room. Rob's grown children and his wife continued to talk about future plans, preceded by unrealistic phrases such as "when Dad gets better." They knew, but were too afraid, to have the conversation in which the words that were in everyone's mind—*terminal, dying*—would need to be spoken. They would need a lot of support and teaching, and this teaching would have to be done in a short period of time, since Rob's disease was advanced.

I arrived at Rob's home the first time with great trepidation. His attractive wife, Emily, met me at the door and confirmed my fears by telling me that Rob had been miserable all night with unmanaged symptoms of nausea, vomiting, and pain, and his abdominal girth was expanding by the day with fluid related to his tumors. My mind was becoming boggled with the difficulties of this case, and I hadn't even met my patient yet.

Emily led me upstairs and introduced me to her husband. I liked him immediately. The way Rob presented himself was a combination of the boy down the block you played with as a kid, your first high-school sweetheart, and your brother. Despite how ill he was, he had a manner and smile that could charm even the grouchiest nurse! We had an instant rapport, and I looked forward to every visit, always arriving armed with a new list of ideas for interventions to alleviate his suffering, which eventually he benefited from and appreciated.

On the good days, we would talk while I massaged his feet with lotion, which he loved. While I rubbed his swollen feet, he would close his eyes and tell me about his experiences as a high-school football coach and as a patented inventor. And he told me about how much he loved his family, especially his two-year-old granddaughter. It saddened him very much that she might not remember him after he was gone, but he seemed to make peace with this by knowing how much she was loved by the rest of the family. Also of comfort to him was his strong belief and conviction that he would still be able to watch over her from heaven after his death.

Rob declined rapidly after the discomfort of his distended abdomen made it too difficult for him to leave his bedroom. He had reached his line in the sand, so to speak. Those of us working in hospice often observe that when patients get to the point that they no longer have the quality of life they need or want for themselves, they appear to "flip a switch" that allows them to give in and let the illness take over. "Giving in" and "giving up" are two very different concepts. The giving in usually occurs well after the fight—the treatments and surgeries designed to extend life, or, in some cases, cure an illness—have been put aside. This is usually a time when patients realize that they would rather be gone than to accept the limited life their disease offers. More often, they come to the realization that there is somewhere better to be than sick in bed. In any case, whether the decision is a mental, spiritual, or emotional one, patients often come to a place of peacefulness in facing the next part of the journey. Witnessing the change that occurs is like watching them shift from driving on a crowded, busy highway to coasting slowly along a county road. However difficult it is for the family, when this giving in occurs, loved ones need to accept this very personal decision of the patient and to let them know they will support it. Rob had reached this point.

I could see that Rob was failing, and with the support from the entire hospice team, we were finally able to get his family to accept his terminal diagnosis. Courageously, with encouragement from the hospice staff, Rob himself drew his family together to share with them how difficult the journey had become for him. By this time, it didn't take a medically trained eye to see how much he had declined, and what his family had previously refused to see was becoming more obvious. Now the family could begin to prepare for his death. His doctor and I had worked hard to manage his symptoms and we achieved success. Rob was finally comfortable and able to settle into a quiet, restful phase. I knew it wouldn't be too long until he died, but I never thought it would be just a day after our last visit, when he had been weak but alert, smiling, and talking.

His death came when I had gone to Wisconsin for a weekend of solitude at our family's cabin in the woods. Heading back home the following day, on a deserted road before getting back on the expressway, I checked my voice-mail log for an update on whether Rob had managed to remain comfortable over the weekend. I heard the voice of one of my nurse coworkers say, "I wanted to tell you that Rob died today. I thought you might like to know before you come to the office on Monday."

Just as I heard the words and started to cry, I drove over a small hill in the road. As I did so, more than two hundred black crows flew up from the road, blackening the sky and flying in circles, and I pulled over to the side, stopping to watch what was occurring above me. I had never seen such a thing. For the next five minutes, as I watched the birds in their air-dance, I paid closer attention to the song that was playing on the radio, and the words being sung were, "When you die, just a little, and cry, just a little . . ."

There was one crow, no larger or smaller than the rest, that appeared to be leading this aerial display, with all the other crows following its joyous movements. "Is that you, Rob?" I wondered. I continued to watch the crows until, all at once, they swooped low, almost to the hood of my car, like a huge black blanket, and then flew off in one large mass over the trees. They seemed to be leaving me a parting gift from Rob, and my heart lightened.

In Native American tradition, by the way, the crow is believed to have the task of escorting souls to heaven and of bringing light to darkness.

Chapter 14

Promises

Ernestine was, as the old poem goes, a jolly old elf, and I became the fortunate beneficiary of having her as my next-door neighbor. By the time we moved into our century-old Victorian house, she had lived in her home for more than four decades. She was ninety-four years old when we met, and she still maintained her own small home and large yard independently, despite a serious heart condition and her advanced age.

My new neighbor was wary of strangers, and it took several months for her to accept that this new family next door meant her no harm and, in fact, wanted to be friends. Once a trusting relationship was in place, she explained to me the reason for her initial hesitation. Ernestine's only son had gone missing in action in World War II. For ten years afterward, Ernestine was plagued with prank phone calls from men claiming to be her son. I was appalled at the cruelty of this action when my new friend told me of the suffering it had caused her. I certainly understood why she held back from people she didn't know.

Over several years, as Ernestine aged ever closer to her hundredth birthday, she became less able to do the more strenuous jobs around her home. Until this time, although neighbors offered to help, she graciously declined and kept up her activity, however slow. We honored her desire to be independent, but also kept watch for small ways we could help.

One day, while Ernestine was digging in her flower bed, she tragically dug into an underground bee's nest. The frantic bees swarmed, stinging her on her face and arms. She was able to climb her porch stairs and into the house, but by the time she was able to call for help she had been stung so many times on her eyes that she became legally blind, just able to see colors and vague shapes.

Navigating outside and caring for her property became impossible for Ernestine, and so her other next-door neighbor and I made a pact. I would cut and maintain the front yard, and he would do the same in the back. Ernestine accepted this offer with gratitude.

Although I never let Ernestine know what day I was going to cut her grass or trim her shrubs, it never failed that, while I was working, I would see her tiny frame come out the front door and wave money at me. Time and time again, I would stop the mower, not only to visit with her, but to decline payment for my favor. During this time, I was in nursing school, and when Ernestine would fret about my not accepting money for the help I was providing, I would tell her, "Just pray me through nursing school."

"That's all?" she would ask.

"That's a *lot!*" I would answer. And I meant it.

Ernestine felt that she had to do more, though. Although I never saw her perform the action, somehow this elderly, sightless elf would make her way down her porch stairs, across both of our properties, and up my own front porch stairs to leave a bag of candy in the mailbox for my children, with a tiny scrawled note of thanks. If I protested that this "payment" wasn't necessary, Ernestine would pretend innocence and say, "I can give your children candy, if I want to, can't I?"

I must say, Ernestine must have had a hotline to heaven, because eventually I was ready to graduate, and with high honors no less! Many members of my family came from out of town for my graduation and pinning ceremonies, which were held on a Sunday afternoon.

That day, I was dressed in my crisply new, white nurse's uniform, with a corsage on my lapel. We were literally piling into the car—my husband, children, sisters, and mother—when suddenly I announced, "I'll be right back; I have to show Ernestine how I look and thank her for her prayers." I don't know what prompted me to do such a thing at the last minute, but I was glad that I did.

I trotted over to my dear neighbor's porch and rang the bell. Within seconds, I heard her frail voice calling, "Oh, help me. Help me."

I ran to the side of her home and found that, sometime earlier in the day, she had fallen from her porch, landing on the ground beside it. Ants were crawling on her, and she had a sheen of perspiration from being exposed to the sun and probably from shock as well. I comforted her for a minute, brushed the ants off of her, and hollered to my family. "Call 911 NOW!"

Within two minutes, the paramedics had arrived to transport her to the hospital. Being familiar with Ernestine's house, I was able to find phone numbers to contact her daughter and a list of medications to help with her hospital admission. I kissed her goodbye and went back to join my family, now much less composed and excited about the graduation ceremony that would take place in less than an hour. We arrived on time, and the ceremony was wonderful, but my heart was with Ernestine the rest of the day.

Ernestine died of complications of her heart condition the next day, at age ninety-nine. I never saw her again.

I often think about the day I found Ernestine lying on the ground in her yard, alone and frightened. What must she have thought when I showed up in the nick of time, dressed all in white, flowers on my lapel, and the full sun shining behind me? Although Ernestine had now been legally blind for many months, she appeared to be "seeing" me with new sight, perhaps that of inner knowing, because when I arrived at her side, her eyes and mouth opened wide in what appeared to be surprise as much as awe, as if she had seen an angel. I will forever hope that, in her panic, this is what she thought, because her frightened expression calmed almost immediately.

I was fairly certain that, on the day of Ernestine's funeral, her family would come over to her house, so, the evening before, I went to cut her grass and tidy her yard. I was mowing a swatch of grass near the street when I looked up and saw that the entire front of Ernestine's house was bathed in golden light. Not my house next door to the left or the other neighbor's house on the right; just Ernestine's house.

When I walked up to the house to determine the source of the light, I noted that the sun was hitting an upstairs window on the house across the street in just such a way that the reflecting beam was bouncing back in a direct line to Ernestine's house. The sight lasted only a few short minutes as the sun set farther into the sky. My feeling was that of Ernestine leaving, after having kept her promise to pray me through my studies, right up to my graduation day.

Chapter 15

Till Death Do Us Part

Margaret met me at the door when I came to visit her sick husband. She was tall and lean and elegant, with a Katherine Hepburn look about her. The woman in front of me had a willowy body, a tidy grey bun on the top of her head, and the clean, pretty look of a girl raised in the country. Margaret's appearance, and the way she moved, belied the fact that she would turn eighty-five on her next birthday. She was in excellent health, she told me, and could care for her husband alone, but her daughters insisted on helping her. I was glad that Margaret had these generous offers from her children. It would allow all of the members of this family time away from their caregiving duties to get a breath of fresh air and to refocus so that they would be able to function for the long run, if that's what it turned out to be.

Doctors give educated guesses about a patient's prognosis—how well they are expected to do with their illness and for approximately how long. However, these patients represent each end of the spectrum; some die much faster, and some live much longer, than the educated guess informs. When an illness goes on for a long time, it can take its toll on the person performing the care. Our concern as healthcare workers is as acute for the person providing the care as it is for the patient.

The caregiving duties are many, and the hours are long, when a patient is succumbing to an illness. Unless there are alternate people to fill in the hours of the care during the day or night, it is truly a 24/7 job. Patients who do not want to be isolated in a bedroom when they are no longer able to be out of bed often opt to place their hospital bed in the living room or other common area so that they can still be in the hub of the home during mealtimes and when visitors arrive. The room becomes a combination bedroom/dining room/hospital room, with portable commodes, extra linens, an over-bed table, a medication table or drawer, stacks of incontinence garments, dressing supplies, walkers or wheelchairs, and many more items that are usually needed to care for the dependent patient.

The duties, which take up a good part of the day, include bathing, dressing, and repositioning the patient multiple times a day. Transfers to a commode at the bedside, or to a wheelchair for trips to the bathroom, can be needed hourly. Frequent diaper and linen changes are an absolute necessity to keep the skin from breaking down into bedsores, and frequent dressing changes to bedsores need to be done, should they occur. Providing meals, glasses of fluid, scheduled medications, and love and support add to the long hours of care. All these combined responsibilities contribute to the common problem of what is known as "caregiver burnout."

Margaret led me to Mason, who was sitting on the sofa in a screen-enclosed porch at the back of the house. Through the screens, flowers and shrubs of every kind could be seen in a panoramic view. Birdfeeders, which attracted dozens of feathered friends, were placed strategically around the yard. The room conveyed the feeling of camping out in the woods, and Margaret and Mason "lived" there during the summer months. They slept out there every night on a pull-out sofa bed, surrounded by a symphony of crickets and other nighttime creatures.

One look at Mason told me that he was very sick and probably only had a few weeks or maybe days to live. His three daughters surrounded him, straightening his collar, kissing him, and talking to him in soft voices. He had oxygen running into a canula in his nose, but still his breaths were ragged. He smiled at me, and all I could think of was one of the elves at the North Pole, with his dove-grey eyes, crinkling at the corners, and his shock of pure white hair. He easily talked about the realization that he was going to die and stated that he was ready. His daughters cried, and Margaret sat beside him patting his back, nodding that she understood.

I noticed that there was no hospital bed in the room and asked Mason if we could have one delivered. Decisively, but kindly, he said, "No, dear. Margaret and I always sleep out here in the summertime, and we always sleep *together*." I simply told him that if he changed his mind to let me know. I completed my visit and told the family I would return after the weekend for my next visit to see if there were any new needs for Mason's comfort.

CHAPTER 15

When I arrived at the home as promised on Monday morning, Mason and Margaret's daughter Katie met me at the door. She had been crying and her face was swollen and red. She said, "Did you hear?"

Although I hadn't received a death notification from our office, I guessed that Mason had passed away, and I said to her, "What time did the death occur?"

Katie answered, "We don't know exactly. We just found her when we arrived this morning."

Her? Katie saw my questioning look and said, "Mom. She died during the night. Dad was lying on his side with his arms around her, and this morning she was gone." I could hardly believe what Katie was saying, until she told me this: "Mom sat us down last night and said to us, 'Girls, you know that I won't be able to live one single day on this earth without your dad, don't you? Please remember that.'" Katie described what else had transpired: that morning, they had moved Mason to another room so that the funeral director could take Margaret's body, but the family didn't know how to tell Mason that his beloved wife had died. Seeing Katie's distress, I volunteered for the task, wondering how I would ever find the words.

Mason was reclining in a chair, his breathing as labored as ever, and he was very pale. It was difficult to rouse him and for him to maintain an alert state for even a few minutes, so I knew that he was getting closer to his death. I took his hands in mine and gently said, "Mason, I have some sad news to tell you. Margaret passed away during the night."

His expression didn't change, and he said softly, "I know. I could feel it when she left. She's waiting for me." I gave a lot of thought to Mason's words, and I wondered at the strong soul connection between two people who were so bonded that one life couldn't go on without the other.

Mason stayed calm and quiet, slowly getting closer to the end of his journey. Throughout the day, Mason could be heard chuckling and talking to Margaret. "Where are you now?" he'd ask. "What's it like there?" He would be silent for a few moments and appear to be listening to the answer. Finally he said, "I'm coming."

Mason's daughters and sons-in-law needed to go to the funeral home to make funeral plans for Margaret and pre-funeral plans for Mason. I offered to stay at Mason's side until they came home. It often happens that dying patients seem to need, or want, to die alone. The evidence is that families or spouses often hold a vigil at the bedside, for days or even weeks, while a patient's death is imminent. When one person gets up from the chair, another sits down, and so someone is always present. The patient often lingers and lingers, with one foot in heaven and one foot on earth, getting no closer to finishing his or her journey. However, if even a brief period is left open when no one is in the room—a bathroom break, or leaving the room to answer the phone—the patient will often take this opportunity to slip quietly away.

Also, very frequently the person who has the closest relationship to the dying person is not the person who is present at the time of death. I have come to think of a patient as having an emotional umbilical cord to the people he or she loves and who also love him or her. When the cords are strong, as when the loved ones are in the room, the dying person sometimes finds it difficult to leave. When there is peace, quiet, and the focus of being alone, or of not being held to their physical body by bonds of love, they seem to be more easily able to drift away. For this reason, we often tell families and loved ones to offer the patient choices: give them some time with you and some time alone, so that they can choose the way they need it to be for the most peaceful passing.

In view of the quiet and surprisingly quick way that Margaret had left her body earlier in the day, I mentioned to Mason's family that they might want to say goodbye to him, even if they were going to be gone only a short time. Each daughter and each son-in-law came to Mason's side, hugged and kissed him, and said goodbye, adding the most important message that the dying need to hear: "We know you need to leave, daddy, and it's okay."

The family wasn't gone for fifteen minutes when Mason's breathing changed to a Cheyne-Stokes pattern, meaning that there were twenty to forty seconds between breaths, a sign that death can occur soon. I stayed at his side for the next five minutes, praying for an easy passing, and then Mason was gone. I called Katie at the funeral home to tell her the news, and she told me she knew when the phone rang what the message would be.

A double funeral was held two days later, and Mason and Margaret were buried the way they had been since they met sixty-five years earlier: together, side by side.

Chapter 16

Upstairs

I had been a hospice nurse for only a few months when I visited my new patient, James. He was a ninety-two-year-old gentleman who spoke with a strong Irish brogue. He had the look of an elderly leprechaun, with crystal-blue eyes and curly, snow-white hair. He was far along in his illness of congestive heart failure and bedridden by the time I became his nurse. His caregiver reported that he was often confused and showed signs of anxiety at times. One day, during my visit, he fidgeted and twitched in his bed. He finally said, in a soft whisper, "I need to go upstairs."

This, apparently, was some of the confusion that his caregiver had reported. I looked around at his tiny, one-story apartment and gently told him, "Your apartment doesn't have an upstairs, Jim."

He quieted then, but at my next visit, he said insistently again, "I really need to go upstairs."

Could he be thinking of his childhood home, or of another place he had lived? I stroked his forehead and his hand and reassured him, "It's okay, Jim, relax. There isn't an upstairs here." Jim seemed close to dying, but several days later he was still lingering and becoming more restless.

As I lay in bed one night, I reviewed all that I had been taught about comfort medications and comfort measures from a medical standpoint. I was certain that I had done everything, covered all the bases, to make Jim comfortable; yet he remained agitated and restless and was obviously lingering in his dying process. Then, like a lightning bolt, I had the thought, "Upstairs! He's telling me he wants to go to heaven!" I barely slept that night, thinking of the one thing that I hadn't provided for Jim: permission to leave. He was waiting for validation of his dying and for permission to go.

When I arrived at Jim's home the next morning, his caregiver reported that he had had a restless night, reaching his hands up into the air and even attempting to get out of bed. I held his hands for a few minutes and then quietly told him, "Jim, it's okay now for you to go upstairs." His restlessness ceased almost immediately; and, within an hour, Jim had climbed the stairway to heaven.

Since those early days of working in hospice, I've witnessed how often people use symbolic language to let others know that they will be leaving soon.

"Make sure you put the strap around my brown suitcase."

"Call the taxi."

"The ship has arrived in the harbor."

"Are my suitcases packed?"

These are all examples of the things the dying tell us as they prepare for their spiritual journey. I believe this is because they are trying to prepare themselves, as well as those they are leaving behind, in language that is gentle and nonthreatening. The appropriate response is to validate that we know they are leaving, which is also a way of giving permission.

"Your suitcases will be ready when you are."

"The ship won't leave without you."

"The taxi will be right on time."

Or simply, "I'm going to miss you."

Expecting to hear and to respond with such statements is something I always teach the families in my care as their loved one approaches the dying process. Invariably, they will later tell me, "You were right!" They are forever grateful for having been able to understand and anticipate this import need of their loved one.

Part Three

Heartwarming Relationships

And in the end, the love you take is equal to the love you make.

—The Beatles

It is always amazing to me to see how some families pull together to support each other during a crisis. However, during the stressful time of a family member's terminal illness, that's not always the case. Many things can disrupt the well-intentioned flow and support of family. Sometimes all the old issues and hurts from the past resurface at this time of raw emotions, and family members divide rather than rallying together. The teamwork necessary in these types of situations can become difficult for numerous reasons: many people are uncomfortable with the sights and smells of illness, or of interacting with someone who is dying, because they don't know how to act or what to say. Instead of rallying together, they choose to stay far away.

In other cases, a family member just can't accept the diagnosis that has come from the physicians. I can't tell you how many times I've gone for a first visit with a hospice patient and a family member—husband, wife, or grown child—will say, "Shhh! Don't tell mom/dad you're from hospice, and don't mention cancer [or ALS/COPD, or whatever the illness might be]." This puts me at a distinct disadvantage, first because my ID badge says "Hospice RN," and second, because that's why I'm there: to help guide them through their physical decline and the dying process when it occurs. Even though I agree initially not to use the "D" word (dying), or to say I work with hospice, I never have taken off or hidden my ID badge. Furthermore, what I have found consistently is that people know they're dying, even if those around them choose to disbelieve it or hide from it. "Alright," I tell the family. "I won't start out talking about cancer or hospice right now."

And do you know what happens? I enter the room to meet my patient, and he or she looks up at me, often smiles, puts a hand out to shake mine, and says, "Hi. I'm Rita. Did they tell you I'm dying of breast cancer?" So, one of the hospice team's most common tasks is to get the words out on the table so that everyone can be prepared, everyone can talk about it, and everyone can relax.

In the following stories, you will meet patients and families whose love for others was both palpable and a joy for those of us who worked with them during their stay in hospice.

Chapter 17

Home Sweet Home

Franklin was a dear little man who had the unfortunate experience of being diagnosed with colon cancer, after already having lived most of his life with rheumatoid arthritis. To complicate the situation, he had married a woman with multiple sclerosis. Despite his own physical limitations, Franklin had been the primary caregiver for his wife until her death several years before Franklin was admitted to hospice.

Franklin belonged to the Jehovah's Witnesses and had a very faith-based way of viewing his own life and the world around him. Adding to his personal charm, he also had a way of seeing even overwhelming issues with great simplicity. His great joy was initiating discussions with those of us who visited him about the wrongs of the world and how he figured, in his simplistic way, he could right them. Because he was homebound with his illness, the Internet became his way of reaching out to the world to give his down-to-earth advice.

Regarding people who were unemployed or down on their luck: "All of that person's neighbors should care for that family by sharing what they have," he told me. "Money, food, shoes, clothes."

Regarding corruption in politics: "Only honest people should be able to be leaders. Someone needs to give them a test about their principles and only allow the honest ones to run."

Regarding war: "If everyone would just put down their weapons for a few minutes and shake hands, they could solve the problem by talking it out."

I don't know how he managed to identify or find them, but Franklin announced one day that he had "emailed all of the bombers and asked them nicely to please spend their money on helping the poor instead of building bombs." His advice might sound silly, but it was pure and simple, the way Franklin saw things.

Franklin lived with his sister-in-law and his nephew after his wife's death, so that is where our hospice staff visited him for the two years when he was declining with his cancer. Four little dogs also lived there: two four-year-old bichon frises named Floyd and FooFoo; an eight-year-old Brussels griffon named Bilbo; and a fourteen-year-old Chihuahua named Cinderella. Franklin loved the dogs more than anything, and he physically struggled to care for them. His arthritis condition made it difficult for him to rise from a sitting position, and his gait was awkward and spastic, making it look like a bizarre dance sometimes. One of my favorite memories is of seeing Franklin in his white, fuzzy, floor-length, terry-cloth bathrobe, sashaying across the room in his strange and wonderful way to let the dogs out or to find them a treat.

The dogs loved him back and crowded around his feet or followed behind in his footsteps, as if he were a pied piper of canines. Franklin was calm about his impending death as far as he was concerned for himself, but he mourned deeply about how his dogs would manage without him. He would cry and say, "The kids [meaning the dogs] won't understand." Leaving them was his one and only regret.

About a month after Franklin's death, I walked into the home of a different hospice patient for a nursing visit. The TV was on, and a daytime show was airing. As I was getting my stethoscope out to begin the visit, I heard the announcer say his guest was Sherry, from the DuPage Animal Shelter. My ears perked up because I lived in DuPage County and both my daughter and my granddaughter volunteer at the shelter. Sherry, the guest, announced that she had brought several pets to show that were presently available for adoption. Suddenly the screen was filled with the fuzzy, funny, mustached face of a Brussels griffon, and I thought, "That looks *exactly* like Bilbo." Sherry went on to say that this dog was eight years old, and his name was—you guessed it—Bilbo! My jaw dropped, and so did my heart. Franklin's beloved dogs, whom he had considered his "kids," had ended up in an animal shelter.

As I walked back to my car at the end of the visit, I remembered that Olivia, the hospice office receptionist, had bought a Brussels griffon puppy several months earlier. She was crazy about Rex and had several friends who also owned this breed of dog. I said a quick prayer and dialed her number. I told Olivia that I knew of a Brussels who badly needed a home and that he had belonged to a recent patient of our hospice organization.

I barely had the words out of my mouth when she said, "I want him!" The very next morning, she and her husband, Dennis, went to tell Bilbo the good news and bring him to their home. We also got information at that time that Franklin's sister-in-law had kept Cinderella and that FooFoo and Floyd had been adopted from the shelter the week before.

I felt that Franklin's story had come full circle and that I had been able to complete something that Franklin hadn't been able to do himself. I imagine him smiling down from his new home in heaven to Bilbo and Floyd and their new homes on earth.

Chapter 18

Now Hear This!

Very often, patients who are dying want to know that those they are leaving behind are prepared for their death. It is always appropriate and beneficial when friends and family members are able to acknowledge the dying process and give their permission for the person to leave. This can be said in a forthright manner, such as "I'm going to miss you when you're gone," or it can be said in a less obvious and maybe less painful way, such as, "Whatever happens, I'm going to be fine." However it is said, the expression needs to be conveyed: "I know you have to go, and it's okay."

I never tired of hearing Bob's stories. He was one of the few surviving World War I veterans in our area, and he had been interviewed by reporters and journalists for his seemingly endless accounts of his and his buddies' activities during the war. His wrinkled old face would come alive, sometimes in tears, as he told and retold tales of the combat he saw in Europe. Bob was talented in many ways: as an architect, a designer, and a builder. He had built his present home with his own hands, and he lived there in elegant comfort with his wife, Vivian.

CHAPTER 18

Vivian was the only eighty-seven-year-old "knockout" I had ever seen outside of Hollywood. She still dyed her hair jet black, had eyeliner and eyebrows tattooed on, and wore only the latest fashions—and only in stark black and white. It frightened her immensely that Bob was sick with cancer, and she had taken a cheerleading approach to his illness. If Bob told her he was tired, she told him, "Well, get up! Get busy! It'll make you feel better!" If he said he had pain, she chirped, "Get up! Get busy! It'll make you feel better!" And if he talked about dying in her presence, she would abruptly get up and leave the room with an excuse of "needing to do something right now."

Bob confided to me at one visit that he didn't "want to die and disappoint Vivian." He told me he thought she would be caught off-guard because she hadn't accepted the fact that he was much sicker now, and I knew he was right. Vivian seemed to be an expert at looking the other way when she didn't like what she saw. No matter how I tried to broach the reality of Bob's decline with Vivian, she would change the subject to gardening, cooking, or traveling. Her denial was so great, despite Bob's obviously failing health, that she fantasized the two of them taking an elaborate cruise together in the spring. To the rest of us, it was easy to see that, for Bob, spring would never come.

Bob was so weak now that he couldn't get out of bed. In fact, he couldn't even reposition himself in bed, and I was assisting him with this task when he spoke. His back was turned to me, and he asked, "Is Vivian here?"

Vivian was standing beside me, and I answered "yes" to Bob's question. I knew that something of great importance was going to take place, and I waited.

Like the soldier he knew himself to be, he commanded an authoritative tone and said loudly, "Now hear this: I have to go. I have to go soon. I can't stay any longer." He paused for a few seconds and went on, "Does Vivian hear me?" I looked at Vivian, whose eyes were wide and whose lips were trembling. There was nowhere for Vivian to run now, and she knew it. I gently moved her closer to the bed and nodded, encouraging her to respond.

Then she put her hand on Bob's shoulder and said, "I hear you. What you said—it's okay." Bob's tense posture relaxed, and in less than ten minutes, he was gone. Like the excellent soldier he was, he had taken the time to prepare his "troops."

Chapter 19

Now I See You

In Rhea's family, everything was discussed and nothing was hidden. Rhea was sixty-seven years old and an avid athlete. Until several months before, she was still running seven miles several times a week, and yet something unexpected happened. She had had an "all clear" mammogram in June, and when she began having right hip pain in September, she saw her doctor. She was diagnosed with breast cancer metastasized to the bone of her hip and to her brain. Since then, she had readily tried radiation and chemotherapy treatments; however, the cancer was aggressively spreading, and she was preparing to die.

I've seen a lot of bald heads in my years of hospice, on women and men alike, and I have grown to think they are beautiful. Never do you see a person's essence as refreshingly naked as you do when they have a bald head. I began to notice that heads come in all shapes and sizes under the fluff of hair that covers them, and without the fluff we each look uniquely similar and drastically different. Men seem to accept their baldness, even if it comes rapidly as a result of illness or treatment, with much less emphasis than do women. Some women cover their baldness with wigs;

others flourish fashionable and colorful scarves in creative ways or simply wear attractive earrings. But Rhea did nothing. And she was strikingly beautiful.

Rhea's family was one of those wonderful families who pull together after learning of a patient's illness. Her husband, in order to maintain their insurance coverage, continued to work during the day and took over Rhea's care in the evening. She had four sisters, and some, if not all of them, stayed every day with her. The brain metastases that came with Rhea's diagnosis caused her to have severe vertigo, or dizziness, and the bone cancer metastases in her hip rendered her unable to walk, so she was bedridden at the time I met her. The first time I went to sea Rhea, all of her sisters were there.

When I walked into the room, Rhea was in bed, and her four sisters had each lifted a corner of the sheet she was lying on and were holding her up in the air, about a foot off the mattress of her bed. I could hear the quiet laughter of the five women as I entered the room. The question on my face must have been clear, because Rhea's youngest sister explained, "Rhea gets stiff from lying in bed. She also wants to experience what it will feel like to 'float' after she dies. So, a few times a day, we hold her up in the sheet." The sweetness of this action went right to my heart.

I didn't know that Rhea's brain tumor had caused her to be 95 percent blind, due to the pressure on her optic nerve. She could detect movement if it crossed her visual field, but she could no longer see. As I approached and introduced myself, she said, "I can't see you. Come closer." She took my hand and drew me very close to the side of her bed, then reached up to my face with both hands. She used her fingers to feel my face, from my forehead to my chin, and all of the areas in-between. When she finished, she smiled and said, 'There. Now I see you." And we settled in for our visit.

At every visit thereafter, I witnessed the same camaraderie and unified support that I had on my first visit. Often one of the sisters would be cooking an elaborate stew or baking a delicious-smelling dessert. Rhea's appetite was very poor, and her body was wasting away, or becoming *cachexic*, as we call it, and she would be able to eat only a few bites of whatever was prepared. But this didn't stop her sisters from trying. If Rhea only engaged in enjoying the aroma, it was worth it to them to cook for her! I would still witness the "floating" exercise at some visits, and always Rhea asked me to come closer so that she could "see" me.

I happened to be on call the night Rhea died. Her family did well, having prepared themselves from the beginning for their loss and knowing that they had made the last months of her life comfortable, loving, and unforgettable.

At 5:00 a.m., I arrived back at home from the death visit at Rhea's house, just in time to see the sun coming up. It was too late to go back to sleep and too early to get ready for work. So I lay in bed, thinking of Rhea and her new journey and hoping that the real "floating" was everything she imagined it would be. Wide awake, and with no mistake, I felt Rhea's fingers trace over the features of my face for the last time.

Chapter 20

Rose Jeanine

When Jeanine died at sixty-five years of age, she was a relatively young grandmother of fourteen grandchildren and the mother of six. Decades before, one of Jeanine's children had been born with multiple anomalies. The child, a boy, had lived until age twelve and died the day after Easter. Every year, this was a memorable day for the boy's parents and siblings. They always spent it together doing something to celebrate the memory of the deceased child.

Even though Jeanine's cancer had advanced to a critical stage, she was awake and alert and enjoyed a beautiful Easter with her family and her younger sister, who had come from California to visit. Jeanine had been up in her wheelchair, sitting at the large dining table with everyone, laughing and enjoying the holiday. In the early hours of the morning, on the day after Easter, Jeanine's condition worsened, and she died—on the same day that her young son had died years before, the same day they had reserved to memorialize him and celebrate having had him in their lives.

All Jeanine's children and their spouses were at her home when she passed away. One daughter had brought her four-week-old baby girl, the newest of Jeanine's grandchildren, to see her before she died. I arrived at the home to provide hospice support shortly after Jeanine's death. I spent time with the family and explained the protocol that needed to be followed. I told them I would go into the kitchen to make the official phone calls while they spent some precious time with Jeanine before she was taken out of the house by the funeral-home personnel. On my way out of the room, I leaned over the baby carrier holding the sleeping baby girl and asked the mother her daughter's name. She answered, "Her name is Rose Jeanine."

As the name Jeanine was being spoken, the baby opened her eyes and smiled a smile wide enough for everyone in the room to witness. It was the baby's first smile, and the family and I were in awe that it occurred on that day, at that time, when her grandmother's name was spoken.

Chapter 21

Birds of a Feather

Our official hospice team, referred to as a "discipline," consists of four persons, each with a different area of expertise in coordinating the care of patients and their families. The stories in *Peaceful Passages* are all from my experience and perspective as a nurse. The nurse case manager is responsible for all the medical care that the patient requires, for acting as the eyes and ears of the physician, for effective treatment of symptoms that are present, and for anticipating any others that might arise as a patient coasts toward their final decline. A large part of the task is teaching previously unskilled, and often reluctant, family members to act as caregivers in dispensing medications safely and performing all the other aspects of home care. The social worker is trained to be a gentle listener, a seasoned counselor, and a liaison between community services and the needs of the family. The chaplain offers a calming presence and spiritual support, no matter what denomination is practiced by patient and family. The nursing assistant uses hands that are invaluable in their gentleness to bathe, dress, and shave patients, and make them comfortable in so many ways.

The lines among those roles often become blurred by necessity. Perhaps it is the nursing assistant who is present, and not the chaplain, when a patient suddenly says, "I'm afraid to die because I haven't been to church in years."

Perhaps it is the nurse who is present, and not the nursing assistant, when a patient says, "I would feel so much better if I had a nice bath."

And perhaps it is the social worker or chaplain who is present, and not the nurse, when a patient reports that he or she is having pain. All the team members work and communicate together to provide continuity and excellence of care.

There is another valuable member of the hospice team whose role can be as integral in a patient's case as the assigned four members, and that is the volunteer. Volunteers come in many shapes and sizes and from all walks of life: the female attorney who gives of her time because she wants to "give back" something she received from hospice while her father was a patient; a young medical student who wants to experience what the death of a patient feels like before she is the doctor diagnosing and treating a patient who is dying; a musician who wants to share her gift of melody with a patient who has little time left to appreciate such things. Our volunteers babysit young children in the family, read to patients at the bedside, cut the hair of home-bound patients, grocery shop for an overwhelmed family, deliver weekly books on tape from the library. No chore is considered too small or too large if needed and desired by a hospice family. Because of their true giving nature, hospice volunteers are very much appreciated and loved by the patients and families they serve.

When Eleanor had a near-fatal stroke at age eighty-four and her condition was deemed untreatable by the neurologist, she was moved from her apartment to a skilled-nursing facility. I walked into her room on that first day and saw her lying in bed with her eyes closed, her face a blank mask. I approached her quietly and tried several techniques to rouse her. Eleanor's eyes never opened and her breathing pattern didn't change, even when I turned her onto her side so that I could assess her skin. At every visit for nearly a month, even though Eleanor didn't respond, I kept up a friendly chatter about the weather, the meal menu, something that I had heard that made me happy or made me laugh. Again, I encourage people who have a family member with dementia or any other cognitive limitation—even someone in a coma—to talk to them as if they were alert. The fact that a person is unable to respond to us doesn't mean that they don't understand what is being said. I can't tell you how many times I've seen evidence of the apparent "fog" lifting, if only for a few seconds, as a previously demented or comatose patient answered or asked a question relevant to what was being said to them or around them at the time.

Eleanor's sister, Mary Lou, was younger than Eleanor by seven years. Mary Lou had been deaf since childhood, and Eleanor had become her protector and best friend. Neither had married or had children. They had lived together their whole lives, up until the time Eleanor had her stroke. Now Mary Lou was in the same retirement complex, but upstairs in an apartment, and Eleanor was in the nursing home where she could receive the care she needed around the clock. I don't know if it was sadder for me to see Eleanor in the locked-up condition of her stroke or to see her lonely younger sister sitting tirelessly at the bedside, day after day, begging Eleanor to wake up.

So slowly that I almost thought I was imagining it, Eleanor did begin to wake up several weeks after her stroke. Eyelids fluttered one day, fingers stretched another day, and then there was the long-awaited smile that Mary Lou and many others prayed for. Initially, Eleanor was slow to process speech and thought, but she began to make steady progress. Mary Lou and I started play word games, spelling games, and other such games with her to challenge her thinking and, sure enough, the fog lifted. Eleanor's physician, who had not seen her since she suffered the stroke, walked into her room to hear us playing a game designed to help Eleanor with word retrieval skills, and he couldn't believe his eyes. After doing a physical assessment, he commented, "Well, Eleanor, it looks like you're getting better!" Eleanor hooked her thumb in my direction and answered with a smile, "Well, you can blame it on *her*."

Although Eleanor's mind improved and her fun-loving personality returned, she was never able to walk or stand again. She had severe muscle weakness in her arms, battled constantly with lung and urinary tract infections, and had frequent TIA's—small strokes that can last for seconds to hours. She was dependent on others for most of her needs, but nonetheless she felt herself fortunate still to be alive. Of course, Mary Lou was ecstatic about what she considered a miraculous change of events.

Around this time, two hospice volunteers were assigned to Eleanor. It has to be said that they were assigned to Mary Lou as well, because with Eleanor and Mary Lou, you didn't get one without the other! On Tuesday mornings, Kathy, one of the volunteers, began a routine of taking Eleanor, in her reclining wheelchair, to a common area called the Gathering Place at the facility where the sisters lived. Kathy would bring baked goods and pull tables together for an impromptu coffee-klatch for whoever cared to stop by. Before long, a dozen or so residents from the complex made it part of their weekly activity to drop by for refreshments and a short visit. Caroline, the second volunteer, began to do the same thing on Saturday morning, always baking some tantalizing surprise for the group. Eleanor and Mary Lou were in their glory! Their volunteers fussed over them and provided an opportunity for socialization and a chance to meet new people in a way they never could have done for themselves after Eleanor's stroke. There were elaborate birthday parties and Christmas get-togethers in this setting as well. The two volunteers became the family that Eleanor and Mary Lou had never had.

Eleanor thrived on this attention to the point that she eventually "graduated" from hospice, meaning that she was no longer in a declining condition and did not fit the strict Medicare criteria to keep her in hospice. She could no longer receive care from me, from the social worker, the chaplain, or the nursing assistant, and we reluctantly said goodbye to official visits with Eleanor and Mary Lou. Her two wonderful volunteers, though, out of the goodness of their hearts, continued to visit them and provide the friendship and socialization that the sisters had come to love.

About eighteen months after Eleanor had been discharged from hospice care, her condition began to change. She was now eighty-nine years old and began the steady decline that often occurs with patients in advanced age. Although the volunteers continued to help Mary Lou organize her group of friends for coffee and cookies twice a week, Eleanor either slept in her chair while the party went on around her, or stayed behind, asleep in her bed, too weak to attend.

The hospice team had plenty of time to prepare Mary Lou for the final loss of her beloved sister and best friend. The Tuesday volunteer, Kathy, moved away from the area two months prior to this time, but she remained in contact by email and telephone calls. Caroline continued to support Mary Lou with her weekly visit, as regularly as clockwork.

And as Eleanor was taking her last breaths one quiet winter day just before Christmas, who was holding her hand, as well as Mary Lou's, as she passed from this world? None other than Caroline, her dedicated volunteer. How blessed hospice organizations are to have these angels, who by their pure generosity give so freely of their time!

Chapter 22

That's a Lotta'

I could smell the aroma of a warm, hearty stew before I even knocked on the door of the small apartment in the Section 8 housing complex. I heard mumbling inside as someone fumbled with the latch, then the door opened.

Standing there was an elderly woman who came up only to my armpits. She was in a housedress and full apron. In one hand she held a mixing spoon, and in the other a potato. The scarf around her head only partially hid the fact that most of her hair was gone, and her skin was the unnatural, sallow color of many cancer patients. Suddenly she smiled, and her whole face lit up. It was the dumpling face of one of those carved-apple dolls and as cute as a button.

"Come in," said Anna. "I got a lotta' food." Anna had been expecting me because I had called the night before to schedule the appointment. Two places were set at her tiny kitchen table. She said simply, "Sit down," and I did. "I know we gotta' do some work, but we eat first." She proceeded to fill our plates with a goulash mixture that was the best I had ever tasted, with thick slices of homemade rye bread on the side. During the meal, I learned that

Anna was from Hungary and that she had one son, Henri, who visited almost every day. She told me that she had been a widow for many years and that, at age ninety-four, she didn't have any friends left. I could sense as she spoke that she was very lonely.

After we ate, I quickly helped Anna clear the table, mindful of the fact that I had several other nursing visits to make before the day was done. I asked her what she knew about her illness. She simply shrugged and said, "I gotta' lotta' cancer." When we moved to the tiny living room so that I could perform the nursing assessment, Anna sat in the only chair in the room, a cozy but worn recliner. As I looked around for someplace to sit, Anna said, "Why don't you sit on my 'American Chair'?" She pointed to the corner. Anna had crocheted a red, white, and blue afghan and used it to cover her bedside commode so that it wouldn't be recognizable as a toilet to visitors who might drop by. I laughed at her resourcefulness, pulled the commode forward, and we completed our visit.

Every visit started and ended the same way. The beautiful meal was served and eaten, then we moved on to the medical part of the visit, with Anna in her recliner and me perched on the "American Chair." At one visit, Anna's eyes clouded and she confided, "I got a lotta' pain." We made several adjustments to her medications with an order from her doctor and, soon afterward, Anna began to fail quickly. She was too weak to live alone, and Henri moved in to take care of his mother. I asked Anna, now bedridden, if she felt that her life was coming to an end. "Oh, I know I don't got a lotta' time," she answered.

At my last visit, I held Anna's hand and rubbed her brow. I thanked her for "a lotta' good meals, a lotta' good fun and a lotta' good love." Anna smiled, understanding my joke, and patted my hand. She was gone in a few minutes, and I have to say I believe a lotta' angels were there to carry her home.

Chapter 23

Male Bonding, in Spirit

Several months after Chuck was discharged from rehab, I started to visit him in his home. At fifty-two, he had been relatively young when he had a severe stroke while on vacation with his family. Even immediate emergency treatment and aggressive rehab could not reverse the damage that the stroke had caused. Chuck would forever be fed from a feeding tube placed in his stomach, speak with garbled words, and be unable to walk or care for himself or to return to any of the activities of a husband and father. Perhaps one of the most distressing outcomes of the stroke had been that Chuck's arms continuously flailed above his head in uncontrollable movements.

To add to this sad outcome was the fact that Chuck's mind was completely unaffected by the stroke. He knew exactly what had happened to his body, to his life, and to the life of his family when the stroke occurred. His wife, Karen, could no longer work, because she needed to be home to serve as caregiver to Chuck. Her parents, Bill and Sonia, moved into Karen and Chuck's home to provide assistance, considering the enormity of the task of caring for Chuck in his post-stroke condition.

There would be a Hoyer lift machine to get him in and out of bed, a stair-chair lift to bring him downstairs, a special mattress to protect his skin, medications, an electric wheelchair, diaper changes, a Foley catheter, tube feedings, and all of the other paraphernalia that was required for caring for someone in Chuck's condition. Karen felt overwhelmed. The limited financial resources they had had were spent on the initial hospital and rehab care and the aforementioned items for Chuck's care, and now there was nothing left to pay a hired caregiver or nurse. Karen and Chuck had two grown daughters, one of whom was a full-time student going to an out-of-state college; the other was married and also living out of state with a family of her own, so their support system was small.

Caregiving duties would begin at 5:00 a.m. when Karen rose to bathe Chuck, dress him, and wait for Bill and Sonia to assist with his Hoyer lift transfer, his lift-ride down the stairway, and then his wheelchair ride into the kitchen for breakfast. Medications would be crushed, the tube feeding would be started, and the rest of the family would sit down to breakfast with Chuck just as if it were any other normal day and normal routine. They laughed, read articles out loud from the morning paper, and talked about plans for their day. Chuck was always included in their conversation, and they learned what his guttural utterances meant, or, at other times, were able to anticipate his needs without his speaking.

In any case, they made a valiant attempt to resume a sense of normalcy in the routine of their day, and this allowed Chuck to feel that he wasn't a burden to them, that he was still an integral part of the family. Karen bought a used handicapped-equipment van and was able, despite the work it took to transport him, to take him along when the family went on outings. Chuck was happy, at least as happy as he could be in his condition, and probably happier than most because of the wonderful care provided by his loving family.

One of the blessings of this forced situation was that Chuck and his father-in-law became very close. Even when Bill wasn't "on duty" for Chuck's care, he would be found sitting next to him during a TV football game, reading him a story, or pushing Chuck around the neighborhood in his wheelchair on a nice day. When Bill entered the room, Chuck's face would light up. Much of the time, Bill would keep up an interesting, one-sided conversation while Chuck listened; but even when they weren't talking, they seemed to share a deep sense of connection, peace, and quiet understanding.

This plan worked like a well-oiled machine for several months, and then disaster struck again. Bill was diagnosed with a fast-growing lung cancer and was told that he had less than three months to live. Now I had two hospice patients in one home. This can happen occasionally, but it is always a doubly sad situation for the family involved, as they know that they will be losing not one, but two, family members in a short period of time. It certainly disrupted the flow of organization that had been put in place in this home, because everyone had an integral role of equal importance in keeping the wheels rolling. Karen and Sonia stepped up to the challenge, in their amazing, organized, hardworking manner, and, with assistance from hospice, began to care for both Chuck and Bill.

Within a few short weeks, Bill was no longer able to perform any of the caregiving that he had provided for his son-in-law; yet when Chuck was settled for a rest after his cares were completed by Karen and Sonia, Bill would be waiting to spend time with him. Often the two of them just sat together quietly. Sometimes a patient's prognosis—how long and how well a patient is expected to do—is way off the mark, but in this case, it was dead center. At exactly the three-month date from his diagnosis, Bill began to succumb to his cancer, becoming weaker and weaker. Now it was Chuck, in his wheelchair, who sat at Bill's bedside. The flailing arms didn't bother either of them, it appeared, and they sat wordlessly and contently in each other's quiet, unassuming company for hours on end.

I arrived for my visit early one day to find our hospice nursing assistant, Milt, bathing Bill in bed. Bill had reached a point of nonresponsiveness over the past several days, and we all knew that he might die at any time. Chuck was still upstairs in bed, and I told Karen that I would do my assessment on him after I helped Milt finish caring for Bill. Just as we were placing Bill on his back and fluffing his pillow, he let out one sigh and was gone. His family wasn't in the room, but they were all at home. I noted the time: 7:55 a.m. I called Karen and Sonia into the room to break the news, and Milt and I spent nearly an hour comforting them and making the official phone contacts required for a death occurring at home.

When Karen felt that she had calmed down and could talk to Chuck, she went up to tell him that Bill had passed away. However, when she entered the room, Chuck had tears on his cheeks and said, in his garbled speech, "I already know. Bill went to heaven at 8 o'clock."

Karen, assuming that Chuck had overheard talking or crying from downstairs, asked, "How did you know?"

Chuck said, "He stopped by my bed to tell me goodbye before he left, and he said that he'd be back to get me when it's time."

After Bill died, Chuck made it clear that he didn't want any aggressive measures taken to prolong his life, including being treated by antibiotics if he got an infection. We promised Chuck that he would be kept comfortable, with no means of attempting to extend his life, when his time came. Several months later, Chuck joined his father-in-law and friend. I wasn't there at the time of Chuck's death, but I believe Bill kept his promise and was there to welcome him home.

Chapter 24

Shared Death Experience

If you have read *Glimpses of Eternity* by Raymond Moody, published in 2010, you will be familiar with the term "shared death experience." Although these experiences vary greatly in their content, there are hallmarks that categorize them. The concept is this: as one person is dying, another is able somehow to fine-tune to the experience on a spiritual level. These occurrences are not as rare as one might think, as I was blessed to experience myself.

I pulled up to the address for my newest patient and felt a bit intimidated by the size of the home and the neighborhood in which it stood. This was a *ritzy* location, all of the houses appearing to belong to the rich and famous. I knew that Roger was only fifty-eight years old and was in end-stage ALS, Lou Gehrig's Disease, and I felt sorry that whatever effort he had made to earn this elegant lifestyle was being negated by his disease process. ALS, even with the finest treatment, usually has a three-to-six-year survival rate, and Roger was in his fourth year. When they say that money doesn't buy the things that *really* matter, this is a fine example.

ALS is a neurological disorder that is not fully understood. Although much research is being done, the cause is still elusive, and treatment is intended simply to reduce and slow symptoms. There is no cure. ALS generally starts in the lower extremities, as it did with Roger, and moves upward, rendering muscles useless. Once it begins to involve the lungs and diaphragm, the disease is in its final throes. Most patients acquire a feeding tube, if that is their wish, but few choose to live on a ventilator when breathing becomes an issue, because the rest of their body is already so wasted away by the disease.

Roger was in bed, where he was now confined twenty-four hours a day, when I met him. Seriously, this guy was drop-dead handsome, and he had a winning smile and a personality to match. He was very engaging, and I understood why he had been such a successful figure in one of the largest corporations in the United States as a salesman and motivational speaker. His wife, Lauren, told me that they had traveled extensively together, both for business and for pleasure. They had led a life of entitlement, although hard-earned, until Roger received his diagnosis.

Roger and Lauren had two sons in high school and an older daughter who was married with a young son of her own. Roger's parents were still alive, and he had two siblings close to his age.

A young person's anticipated death always feels so out of order. *No* parents expect to bury their children, and young children and wives don't expect to lose their father and husband. Somewhere along the journey, the people involved in this unexpected scenario have to make sense of it in whatever way they can. This family was doing the emotional work, sadly but necessarily, and they were slowly gaining acceptance that Roger would die.

On most visits, I would have to vie for time alone with Roger. A steady stream of former corporate colleagues, family members, golf buddies, and neighbors were always arriving for a chance to visit with this man with the effervescent personality. They came to make *him* feel better, but somehow the reverse often happened and the guest left feeling enhanced. This was the effect that Roger had on people in his presence. He certainly did on me. Although I was there to provide medical care and comfort, I often wondered if I was doing as much for him as he was for me.

This is not to say that there were no bumpy roads. Roger had moments of anger and depression and blame when his illness got the best of him, which made the task of caring for him even more overwhelming. For a while, he would coast along with no problems, on a steady plateau; then suddenly his condition would drop a few notches, and his whole routine would have to be revamped to accommodate the new level of care. Initially, Lauren was his primary caregiver, and, for a woman with a petite frame, she was very strong. But soon transferring Roger to the toilet or electric wheelchair became impossible for her, and a part-time caregiver who learned to anticipate Roger's needs was hired to help.

Roger already had a feeding tube and was completely paralyzed, except for the forefinger on his left hand. An apparatus had been designed and set up to allow him to use this one finger to operate a computer so that he could still be involved in his business operations and, in his isolation at home, be in contact with friends via the Internet. Many times, Roger would spend whatever time it took to type in a message of greeting for me when I arrived for my nursing visit. In a mechanical, robotic voice, the message would be delivered by the push of his forefinger, and the rest of us would howl at whatever crazy nonsense Roger had "said." Sometimes it was a short poem: "Here comes a nurse, carrying a purse; I hope I'm not worse!" Sometimes it was a joke: "Sorry if I seem tired; I played twelve holes of golf today." And sometimes it was simply jibberish—"Razz-a-ma-tazz, du-bop, ring-a-ling, BAM!" Coming through the automated voice of the computer, these things sounded hilarious.

In just over one year's time, I saw ALS steal Roger's ability to speak, to smile, to hold his head up, to breathe on his own, or to be able to have bodily processes function without intervention. Finally the disease hit home: Roger's lungs were being paralyzed. He had a stimulator surgically implanted into his diaphragm to help this powerful muscle stay strong, but it became useless after a while. Eventually, he was put on a machine with a mask called a BIPAP that helped his lungs to inflate when they could no longer do the job unassisted. When he could no longer speak, his family and I learned his code of eye blinks that told them yes or no to questions they asked.

Although he was rarely left alone, there were times when he had to be, and so a preprogrammed cell phone was left in his left hand where he could push a button for help if he needed or desired something. Roger's musculature was so flaccid that if the head of his bed was up an inch too high, his head would flop forward like a rag doll, and he would be unable to reposition it without hands-on assistance by the person caring for him. Roger had the best of the best, the best money could buy in equipment, medical care, hired help, and medication, but he was still dying from ALS.

Those big brown eyes. Even though his mouth couldn't smile or communicate, his eyes still did. I saw appreciation, teasing, humor, disappointment, and sadness in those eyes. Roger knew that his time was getting short.

I often dream of my patients, and so it was not unusual for me to dream about Roger one night after visiting him. But this dream was different; it was a lucid dream and had the distinct quality of being as real as if it were actually happening. I dreamed that I was in Roger's bedroom, sitting next to him on his bed, while a party was going on around us. There were lots of people there whom I had met on other visits to Roger's home, and some I had never met. I saw Lauren, as the hostess of the party, walking around greeting people and offering refreshments. Glancing at Roger, I saw that his color had changed, and despite the BIPAP machine and mask being on, his breathing was becoming labored. I spotted Lauren and called to her, "Lauren, come quick, something is happening to Roger."

In the dream, Lauren appeared not to have heard me and continued her hostess duties. I looked back at Roger and saw that, even in a few short minutes, his condition had deteriorated. I didn't want to leave his side, even for a second, so I called louder to his wife. Still, she didn't hear me and moved farther away until she was out of my sight.

In my dream state, I knew it was now or never, and I turned to Roger, whose eyes were wide open with questions and fear. I took his hands and said to him, "Just look into my eyes. You're okay. Don't be afraid." He calmed down somewhat and I tearfully told him, "You're dying, but when you get there, Roger, it's going to be *so* beautiful!" He communicated understanding with his eyes by blinking once slowly, his head slumped forward, and the mask for his BIPAP machine slipped off. I knew he had died. Then suddenly, unexpectedly, he lifted up his head—something he hadn't been able to do for many months. His face was filled with shining, golden light. He smiled the most beautiful smile I had ever seen and exclaimed in utter amazement, "You're right! It's so . . . very . . . beautiful!" I had never in my life seen a look of such rapture, a look that displayed a thousandfold the beholding of something exquisitely beautiful. His face glowed with reverence and appreciation of whatever it was he was witnessing.

I woke to the phone ringing before my alarm went off. It was a call from Beth, the hospice nurse who had been on call overnight. She reported that Roger had died during the night. While I cried, she told me the story: Lauren had gone upstairs to tidy up the house before going to bed and was unavailable to Roger for a short time, although his phone had been placed in the usual spot next to his fingers. When she came back downstairs fifteen minutes later, Roger was sitting up in bed as she had left him; his head had fallen forward, however, and the mask had slipped off, just as I saw in my dream.

My own experience of this death was profound, and I'll never forget the dream encounter itself or my gratitude for somehow having taken an important role in Roger's dying. I take comfort in the belief that, when he died, he actually did behold the beauty and awe that he conveyed to me in my dream.

Part Four

Mysterious and Spiritual Experiences

Isn't life strange?
A turn of the page,
A book without light,
Unless with love we write.

To throw it away,
To lose just a day,
To the quicksand of time,
You know it makes me want to cry.
—Moody Blues

Grace; presence; glory. Call it what you will. But absolutely call it beautiful when the sacredness of dying comes into your awareness and experience. Nothing I have ever known in this life can compare to the essence of Spirit or the palpable presence of the Divine coming so close that you can almost reach out and feel it.

Many people, even those who would claim to be nonbelievers, discover that being in the presence of the dying makes a change in how they feel—physically, emotionally, and spiritually—right down to their core. It's as if one is standing in a doorway between worlds: one, our own, which we know intimately; and another that we can only glimpse with our hearts and souls. Those moments are humbling, to say the least, with potential to open new doors in the hearts and minds of those who have previously not been aware of the sacred space of dying.

Watch for it. Pray for it. And be in awe when it happens.

Chapter 25

Penny from Heaven

The death of any person, no matter the age or circumstances, is difficult for those left behind. No matter how much preparation one has to face the event, it is never enough for the actual loss when it occurs. If the relationship had been close, missing the person is what's the hardest. If the relationship had been strained, it's the loss of the opportunity for it to have been something else, something better. There might even appear a sense of guilt or remorse, a wishing that things had been different, that one had done more—that one had *loved* more.

I think the most difficult grief, however, is that of a parent when losing of a child. No one expects to outlive their children, especially before the children reach adulthood. It becomes not just the loss of the special person the parents brought into the world, but the loss of so many hopes and dreams.

Bryan was only eighteen years old when he died. He and his mother had shared a special bond; understanding and remembering that closeness made it easier for her to bear her grief most of the time. She was a spiritual person and usually felt strengthened by the time that she spent praying after Bryan died. But one day, her strength was gone. She missed her son and began to feel anger. She turned her anger into a prayer of sorts and cried, "Why Bryan? How could you do that? I don't understand!" She wept for a long time, in a way that she hadn't allowed herself to do since her son had passed away.

Having spent her anger and energy, but feeling lonely and empty, she went to the local supermarket. She remembers every detail of what happened next. She says that she was standing in the pudding section of the store and looked up to see a middle-aged man about six feet away who was staring at her intently. He had a hat on, a slight beard, and the bluest eyes she had ever seen—except for those of her son, Bryan. I can attest to that blue, since I had visited Bryan during his illness: he had eyes the color of clear, Caribbean waters, exactly like those of the man she was meeting now. Bryan's mother felt uncomfortable momentarily and looked away.

When she looked up seconds later, the man was standing very close to her, holding his hat. A single tear rolled out of one of his crystal-blue eyes and down his cheek. He said, "You look as if you are missing a part of yourself." She immediately thought of the answer she always gave when well-meaning friends would ask how she was coping after Bryan's death: "I feel as if I'm missing a part of myself."

The man held out a coin and placed it in the palm of her hand. She looked down and turned it over to see that it was inscribed, "In Jesus, all things are possible." She began to cry silently and looked up. The man who had given her the coin was no longer beside her, nor was he anywhere in sight.

Bryan's mother has the coin to this day, and she knows that her son, or another messenger, was sent to her with this special healing gift just when her despair was the greatest.

Chapter 26

Two People, One Dream

At age eighteen, Michael was too young to die. An honor-roll student, well-liked by his high school peers, and a football captain who had only just begun a talented career, he held very promising potential. Yet dying he was; how could this be? As he lay in a coma, succumbing to the brain tumor that was stealing his life, his mother relayed the following story to me.

When Michael was only two years old, his mother had had a dream. In the dream, she remembers "caring for Michael as an adult in bed, the way a nurse would care for him."

A few years later, she had the same dream, in which the sunlight was pouring into a room that was not familiar to her as she cared for her son.

This dream, without a single detail being changed, came yet again about five years later.

To her surprise, when Michael was about twelve years old, he awoke one morning and told his mother that he had had the very same dream, right down to the detail of the sunlight, which he said "lit up the room." Neither of them could identify the room in which this dream took place. Sometime later, the family moved to a new house in a neighboring community. Shortly thereafter, Michael was diagnosed with an inoperable brain tumor, and, too soon after that, he lay dying. For practical purposes, Michael's hospital bed was set up in the den, providing more space for visitors and easier access for his care.

As Michael's mother gently bathed him in bed in the late hours of the afternoon one day, the setting sun cast its brilliant glow through the west end of the French doors in the den. After a startled moment, his mother told me that they looked at each other with complete understanding and said, "This is the dream."

Michael died several weeks afterward. Although his death was difficult for his mother to bear, she knew, without a doubt, that it was not random, but by design, and that God, in his graciousness, had given them both means of preparation for the difficult task that would be required of them in the future.

Chapter 27

Carpenter Angels

Betsy had been fighting incurable cancer for six years. The disease had traveled from her uterus to her liver and her bones, but she kept fighting. She was receiving chemotherapy and radiation as "palliative care." This meant that these treatments were intended to reduce symptoms and promote comfort, but not cure the cancer, because Betsy's disease was beyond curing. Although the interventions were ravaging her beautiful hair, her appetite, and her ability to stay awake for more than a few hours at a time, she wanted to continue them. "Maybe this time it will work," she told me hopefully at my first visit.

I never take away hope, nor do I give false hope to my patients. Right then, I said a quick prayer that Betsy's needs would be taken care of in whatever way God saw fit to meet them.

Betsy's only child, and her primary caregiver, was her son, Jack. He stayed home to meet his mother's needs during the day, taking her to the hospital and to chemotherapy appointments, and he was attending a local college at night. They lived in an old clapboard home with a steep set of stairs off the front porch. Jack and a friend had built a small ramp because Betsy could no longer walk and Jack needed her wheelchair and the ramp to take her out of the house. Anyone could tell that the ramp was truly a project completed by unskilled hands, no matter how pure the intent. It had no rails or sides, was frighteningly narrow and much too steep. The wheelchair felt like a runaway train with Betsy in it; and in wet or icy weather, it was downright dangerous. More importantly, the city had sent a letter stating that it was not built to code and would have to be removed.

Jack agonized over the ramp. He and his mother were in dire straits financially; and at twenty-two years old, he didn't have the know-how to build a new ramp with the complicated six pages of specifications that the city demanded. He posed his problem to me during one of my visits, and I promised I would confer with the hospice social worker and volunteer coordinator to see if there was a way we could help. After several weeks, there wasn't a single lead as to who might be able to tackle the building of the ramp or how it might be financed, although many people had been contacted in an effort to provide this service to the family.

Betsy revoked from hospice care for a few weeks because she had decided to try more aggressive treatment—yet another type of chemotherapy—and we lost contact during that time. Eventually, and sadly, it was apparent that her new treatment wasn't effective, and she was enrolled once again in our program. I was very sorry to see, at my first visit, that Betsy was now actively dying. She was rarely awake and no longer taking food or fluids. I knew, and Jack knew, that it would be only a matter of days until she was gone.

Jack walked me to the front door at the end of my visit and gestured to the brand-new, completely finished, safe, built-to-code ramp leading up to the front door that I had noticed upon my arrival to Betsy's house. Then he said, "I can't thank you enough for sending the workers to build the new ramp. They showed up and had it done in a day, and I've been able to get my mom to the hospital for treatments or out for walks on the nice days. She was thrilled with the new ramp. Thank you so much." Now I was confused.

When I reached my car, I phoned both the social worker and the volunteer coordinator to see who they had found to build the ramp. They were both surprised by my question. Neither had been able to find anyone to take on the project.

Who were these angels with hammers and saws who had given Betsy the gift of being able to leave her home to enjoy those final weeks of her life? We will never know.

Chapter 28

Barrett's Song

Sometimes it's what the dying person tells you that gives you pause to think and try to comprehend, and sometimes it's what you see or hear yourself. In any case, I've been given many a chance to ponder occurrences that have left me speechless.

Barrett was such a great guy. He was fun, funny, and caring. He and Maureen had been married only one year, although they had dated for twelve years before they married. They spoke their vows on the day before Barrett went for brain surgery to assess a life-threatening tumor. They chose to marry on that day because they wanted to express to each other that they were "in this together." The news after the surgery was not good, and Barrett was sent home to prepare for his death.

I liked both of them the minute I met them. They were very much in love and had a strong spiritual connection that would become even stronger on this last journey they would take together.

When Barrett became very sick and was sleeping much of the time, Maureen told me that he would wake and ask her repeatedly, "Do you know how to fix the digital lenses?

Have you learned how to repair the camera cables?" He would point to different corners of the ceiling as he asked these questions, and Maureen didn't know what to make of the questions. Usually she would comment to him that there were no cables, and nothing needed fixing, but a little later he would ask something similar.

Knowing that he was likely speaking in the symbolic language that dying persons tend to use when their time is getting short, I told Maureen, "I think he wants to know that you'll be okay, that you feel you can handle things when they come up, even if he's not here to help you." I encouraged Maureen to reassure him, symbolically, if necessary, that she could manage. The next day, when the same questions came up, Maureen said to him, "Barrett, have you ever known me not to be able to figure my way out of a problem? I can work the cables, the lenses, and whatever else comes along."

Barrett smiled, went to sleep, and never asked the questions again.

Another day, Barrett said, "Maureen, my mother is standing in the corner. She says hello."

Now, Barrett's mother had been deceased for years, but Maureen dutifully turned to the corner and said, "Hello." Then she said to Barrett, "I think she's here because she's worried about you."

Barrett faced the corner, appeared to listen for a moment, then said tenderly to his wife, "No . . . she says she's here because she's worried about *you*."

Barrett got steadily weaker and was sleeping almost all of the time, finding it difficult to even whisper in the rare moments that he awoke. The day before his death, as I was taking his blood pressure, he opened his eyes wide, looked around the room, and announced clearly and reverently, "Oh my! Oh, MY!" Maureen and I stood by quietly, waiting for what would come next.

Barrett then reached up and placed his right hand under his chin, tapping lightly with the back of his fingers. He began to sing a melody without words, a type of hymn, in what can only be described as the voice of an angel. I was there to witness it: the voice that came out of Barrett's mouth that day was not Barrett's voice; and, to this day, I can clearly remember the incredibly beautiful sound.

I was blessed to have been witness to the events that Barrett experienced and shared with us during his dying. I will always feel privileged to have been present during those very personal and wondrous moments. It is so important for me to let my readers know that these same miraculous occurrences can take place at any death, to any person, no previous experience required! It is simply a matter of allowing oneself, in these most sacred moments, to be open to the Amazing Grace that is present during dying.

Chapter 29

Two by Two

Often, those who are going through the dying process will feel a sense of needing to hang on, not for themselves, but for those whom they love or who love them. I've heard this expressed in many ways, such as:

"I don't want to let my family down."

"I don't want them to be sad."

"I don't know if they understand that I'm going to leave."

In some cases, loved ones have begged the dying person not to leave, stating that they won't be able to go on without them or saying that if their loved one dies, they want to die, too. This is an immense amount of pressure to place on someone who has no choice: the body is dictating that it can no longer function, and the dying process is already in place. Hospice personnel gently help family members find acceptance of the death that is in progress. In addition, they are often able to help loved ones verbalize a message of acceptance that gives the dying patient the needed permission to leave and relieves worry about those being left behind. This acceptance allows the process of dying to unfold with as little emotional upset as possible to the patient. Some family members will be able to "tell it like it is" by saying, "Gosh, mom, I'm sure going to miss you when you're gone." Others can give the same message with different words, such as, "No matter what happens, I'm going to be okay." When this permission of sorts is granted, it is clearly a turning point for many dying persons, and they are able to move forward in their journey unencumbered with a heavy mind or a heavy heart.

My patients are *all* special, but one lady really drew me in. Cancer had invaded much of her body; radiation and chemotherapy had ravaged the rest. She was skeletal from being unable to take hydration or nutrition, and her skin had turned a deep yellow from damage to her liver. She had unnatural fistulas, or openings, draining fluid from tumors in several parts of her body. Yet, she hung on.

I knew that Wanda had a strong faith and that her family had done the difficult but necessary task of giving her permission to go home to God. I wondered why she continued to linger. On one of my visits, while I was bathing her, I wondered out loud, "Why are you still here, Wanda, when you seem so ready to go?"

Although Wanda was minimally alert at the time and hadn't spoken for days, she opened her eyes and whispered, "I want to go, but I have been told that I have to wait . . . that I'm to take someone with me." Hearing this, her family became upset and nervous, wondering if Wanda was referring to someone else in the family who might be about to die. Wanda's statement fueled questions I had never considered. Do we always go in pairs? Do we sometimes need to "escort" others who might not know the way—perhaps infants or people who have never had the opportunity to learn about God or heaven? Wanda sank back into an unresponsive state before I could question her about her comment and never regained consciousness.

At long last, Wanda died peacefully on a Friday night at 7:00 p.m. I called her physician the next morning to inform him of her death. He gave his condolences and then remarked, "Isn't that strange? I had another female patient the same age, with the same diagnosis, who died last night at exactly the same time."

For all the knowledge we *do* have of the dying experience, Wanda reminded me that there is so much more that we don't know. From the visions, concepts, and feelings that patients have shared, it is obvious that they have access to a whole other-dimensional experience that we, whose final moments of life have not arrived, are not able to glimpse. It is also obvious that we are encouraged to understand it. After all the years I have spent at the bedside of the dying, my belief system embraces, with absolute certainty, the understanding that I have nothing to fear of the moment when I will pass from this life to what waits beyond. I view it as an extension, even a bridge, to the next experience. I am forever grateful to all the patients who have given me this understanding through their own encounters with dying.

Chapter 30

By Special Invitation

I was on the fourth floor of the large, county nursing home when my cell phone rang. I glanced at the caller ID and noted that the call was from Lisa, the admissions nurse for our hospice. I knew that she was also present at this facility today, assigned to complete an admission on a new patient whom I would add to my caseload. When I answered the call, Lisa asked, "Janet, can you spare a few minutes to come down to the third floor to meet your new patient, Walt? His whole family is here and they would like to meet the nurse who will be caring for their father."

Within a few minutes, I was able to steal away to fulfill the request. I am always thrilled to meet new patients who come into my care for hospice. I also know how important it is for the family members of these patients to begin a trust relationship with the nurse at the beginning of this difficult period. The sooner this trust is in place, the sooner most family members, as well as the patient, are able to begin the process of letting go.

I knocked at the door of room 1127 and entered. Standing in a straight row in the center of the room were two men and two women, who, I would learn from Lisa's introduction, were Walt's daughters and their husbands. In the bed, on the right side of the room, Walt sat looking over the top of his glasses at me with a smiling, welcoming expression. He held a paperback book in one hand and a can of lemonade in the other. The feeling I got from his family was one of warmth and caring. I felt blessed. I knew that I would love working with this man and the people who so obviously loved him.

Lisa made introductions all around, and then I sat on the edge of Walt's bed. I made light conversation by asking about the book he was reading and if he was hungry for the lunch meal that was about to be served. Finally, I took his hand in mine, gave it a squeeze, and told him that I would return the next day for our first visit together. Walt graciously said goodbye, and I made my way back to the fourth floor to continue visiting other patients while Lisa completed Walt's admission paperwork.

Barely fifteen minutes had passed before Lisa called again. Sounding a little bit hesitant, she said, "You won't be getting Walt as a patient after all." There was a long pause. "He just died." I was stunned. This smiling, adorable man who was drinking lemonade and discussing a book fifteen minutes earlier was gone? Then Lisa proceeded to enlighten me on the sequence of events that had transpired after I had left the room.

Walt's family had departed only minutes after I had, so that Walt could enjoy his lunch without interruption. Lisa had been sitting at his bedside completing her assessment forms when Walt quietly and apologetically said, "I'm sorry. You'll have to leave now." Surprised, Lisa repeated the request. "You want me to leave, Walt?" Walt looked at her solemnly and said, "Yes, please." Lisa, willing to honor his request, stood, began gathering her things and asked simply, "Is there a reason that you want me to leave?" Walt announced plainly, "They've come for me."

Lisa, intrigued, leaned toward Walt and whispered, "Walt, who has come for you?" Walt then turned to his left and extended his arm toward what appeared to be empty space beside him and said reverently, "This is my wife, Audrey." He then extended his arm further and whispered reverently, "And this is Our Lord."

Lisa knew from her assessment interview with Walt that, although he was in the final stages of cancer, he was not confused, disoriented, or befuddled. His conversation and answers to her questions had hit the mark every time. He had answered every question independently and without hesitation. His family had affirmed that the information he gave was correct. Lisa also knew that Walt was a widower, as his wife had died two years earlier.

Obligingly, Lisa picked up her nursing bag, folders, and papers and moved to the desk at the nurse's station to tie up the few loose ends of the admission. It took her no more than fifteen minutes to do so. When she was finished, she went to Walt's room to say goodbye, thinking that, if he was sleeping, she wouldn't wake him.

But when she got there, Walt was already gone, having died in the short time since she had exited his room. They had indeed come for him.

Chapter 31
Remote Connection

Eugene was the most progressive ninety-three-year-old I have ever met. He abhorred taking prescription medications because of the multiple side effects that each one produced. Anyone who has had any sort of prescription filled knows that the printed list of side effects the pharmacy provides is lengthy and frightening. Even simple, over-the-counter medications like Tylenol are associated with contraindications and potential problems: the benefit versus the burden. Eugene diligently investigated naturopathic remedies and was able to replace a lot of his prescription medications with natural supplements, which produced very good results for him. He was also vigilant about his diet and wanted to nurture his body with wholesome intake in every way available. Because he was homebound, his daughters, Carol and Kathy, and his live-in caregiver, Harriet, made sure that all these things were available to him.

Even at his advanced age, Eugene was an avid reader, and he was savvy and conversational about most current issues. He could speak informatively about politics, the economy, weather patterns, and worldviews. He was an expert and interesting source of information on World War II, because he was a veteran with active duty experience.

Energy healing was also an interest of Eugene's, and he kept a satin bag of crystals and stones for healing and for the treatment of his multiple health conditions in his pocket and under his bed at all times. Upon learning that I have been trained as a Therapeutic Touch practitioner, he rarely let me leave a visit without performing a treatment on him. Although Therapeutic Touch is done working mostly with a person's energy field and not touching the body itself, Eugene was sensitive enough to be able to feel the motions of my hands and where they hovered over his body, even though his eyes were closed and my hands were several inches from his skin. "Circles," he'd say, "You're making circles." Or when I was working over his back, "That's the spot. Right near my shoulder."

Eugene's hospice diagnosis was heart failure, and with this condition there are many ups and downs, or what is referred to as a "saw-tooth pattern," which is very difficult for the patient as well as for the family. A patient begins to fail with symptoms of lethargy, shortness of breath, and decreased responsiveness, and it appears that the end is drawing near. But the body somehow shifts its load and recovers, only for the same thing to happen again in a short period of time. Family members get ready for one thing to happen—the actual death—but another thing occurs. This can be emotionally challenging and draining on everyone. I can't tell you how many times this pattern repeated itself over the short time that Eugene was in hospice. Although we all wanted this interesting and lovable gentleman to stay with us as long as possible, we knew that it was only a matter of time before the real event was upon him.

It would be appropriate here to mention the "rally" that is talked about in relationship to the dying experience. A patient who has been declining with almost any disease process may suddenly wake up to a brand-new energy that hasn't been available to him or her for weeks or months. The fogginess of their confusion or sleepiness may retreat, and their appetite may increase to its pre-illness status. They may suddenly feel like they want to get out of bed, or out of the house for an adventure that a week ago would not have occurred to them because of their overwhelming fatigue. They may appear, very suddenly, to be getting stronger or getting better.

One can expect such a rally to be short-lived. The impression of those of us who witness this phenomenon on a regular basis is that the body throws everything it has into a "one last hurrah." When a person is ravaged by disease, or failing with old age, it is unlikely that the burst of energy can continue for very long. Usually, within a day or two, the body settles back into the decline from which it has emerged for this short time and begins the dying process. It isn't always easy to recognize the rally when it's occurring, because it may not appear as profound as the way I've described. But hindsight will usually clarify that a rally did indeed occur. Many families will tell me, "You know, looking back, I can see that my mom had two or three days in a row when she was like her old self just before she died." That's the rally. In any case, another gift from the dying is that we are able to enjoy even the temporary emergence of the person we have known and loved.

One Saturday, when one of Eugene's daughters was out of town, the other was at a family event, and Harriet was off for the weekend, Eugene's condition again began to fail. His substitute caregiver, Donna, was caring for him that weekend, and she saw what we all had seen numerous times before in his condition and his behavior. She kept him in bed that day for both safety and comfort, and observed his decreasing responsiveness, increasing confusion and shortness of breath, and the other clinical symptoms of heart failure.

Late in the evening, Eugene picked up the remote to his TV, which he kept beside him in bed. Instead of changing the channel with it, he held it up to his ear. Then, using it, he made a call to his wife in heaven. Eugene carried on a one-hour conversation with his deceased wife, Mildred. Donna took notes of his conversation for his daughters, and the things she heard him say indicated no signs of confusion at all.

Eugene told his wife that Kathy was on a much-needed vacation and how pleased he was about Carol's new job. He talked about how fatigued Harriet was becoming with his ever-increasing care and said she needed some rest. He told her that he always goes down to the dining room for hot cocoa, but yesterday he swore it was the best cup of cocoa he ever had! Eugene would pause in his conversation, as if listening, and he would chuckle. Over and over again he said, "I'm ready, everything else is in place, and I'm coming soon."

Several times, after Eugene appeared to be listening through the television's remote control device, he laughed and said, "I told you, I'm coming! Keep your pants on!" He spoke of memories of eating hot dogs outside with his family and of other events that had taken place when his girls were small. Often, he would say something that appeared to be in response to a question. "Really? Do you think so?" then he would attentively listen to an answer that only he could hear.

After an hour, Eugene became weaker and the hearty conversation turned to mumbling and half-finished sentences. Donna gently took the "phone" out of Eugene's hands, and they prayed the Lord's Prayer together. Donna tucked Eugene's covers around him and told him to get some sleep, and he replied, "Okay. You sleep, too."

Donna awoke several hours later to find that Eugene, true to his word, had kept the date with Mildred that he had promised.

Chapter 32

Laughing Jesus

Rudy was a slightly built, red-haired gentleman who had a quick and ready smile for everyone, even when he knew he was dying. His wife, Lorraine, was bereft to be losing the love of her life, but she was putting on a brave face for her beloved husband.

Invariably, when I would come to visit, Rudy would be poring over his Bible. He would pull me excitedly to his side and read a passage to me; then he'd close the book and exclaim, "Noah! I'm going to meet Noah!"

The next time I visited, it would be "Moses! I'm going to be in the same place as Moses! The *real* Moses!" He would beam at me and shake his head as if unable to believe his good fortune.

This faith gave Rudy great joy and developed in him a certain anticipation—an urgency, even—about his journey of dying. What awaited him after his death was as real to him as where he was now.

One day, after discussing a Bible story with him, I happened to ask him if he had ever seen the picture of the "Laughing Jesus." The picture I referred to is one of Jesus with his head thrown back and his eyes crinkled shut, and it appears as if he is enjoying a huge belly laugh. I love this picture, as it is entirely different from all of the standard, solemn ones so commonly seen. Rudy had never seen the picture, so I made a copy of mine and brought it to him on my next visit. He stared at it with tears in his eyes and said, "Yes! *This* is the Jesus that I want to meet!" Rudy had me tape the picture to the wall opposite his bed so that he could look at it often.

Lorraine called our hospice one night soon afterward to say that Rudy had died. I arrived at their home in the early hours of the morning to pronounce him and to take care of the other matters that need tending to when a patient dies at home. A tearful but incredulous Lorraine met me at the front door and, without saying a word, pulled me into the room where her beloved husband lay. Rudy had died sitting up in bed, looking at the "Laughing Jesus," with a huge smile on his face.

Chapter 33

Reaping What You Sow

Norman spent a lifetime learning, and then teaching, theology. He infused not only the teaching but the passion of the subject into thousands of willing students over the course of his career.

I met with Norman's son and his wife for a hospice evaluation on a Monday morning. Although I had not assessed Norman, I could tell by the report his family was giving me that he would not be here for very long. He had end-stage Alzheimer's and was losing ground week by week—the Long Goodbye, as it is called. Once Alzheimer's patients start to resist being fed, the road home is a short one. It appeared that Norman was well along this path, and so he was admitted to hospice that day.

Norman had a fairly easy time with his final decline. For the most part, we had not had to intervene with medications for symptom management except to treat a low-grade fever, likely due to dehydration. There was no pain, no anxiety, and he experienced only a little of the labor in breathing that is associated with the dying process. He was bathed and repositioned for comfort, and his family of his wife and five children visited most of the day,

CHAPTER 33

The Violet Hour

y for three days, going home at night to get some much needed rest.

Although not all patients require medical intervention for symptom management, nurses use many adjunctive therapies to promote comfort. Simple interventions such as quiet, calming music playing in the background, a light massage, and Therapeutic Touch to promote relaxation can have a wonderful effect on the mind and body of someone who is dying. Many years ago, I intuitively began to use a dab of violet-colored oil, containing violet and lavender essences with aromatherapy effects, on dying patient's foreheads to promote relaxation. The color violet is also associated with transitions of all kinds and very much so in regard to the dying process. Sometime after I started this practice and began to see its effectiveness, I read, to my surprise, that Florence Nightingale did the same thing for soldiers during the Crimean War, promoting comfort and peace with this practice that, in fact, goes back to ancient times.

On the fourth day of Norman's decline, I arrived at the nursing home in the morning to check his status and make sure he was comfortable. When I entered the room, our hospice chaplain, Father Paul, was standing at the bedside praying Psalm 23. "Yea, though I walk through the shadow of the valley of darkness, no evil shall I fear. . . ."

I walked to the other side of Norman's bed and laid my hand on his arm and began to pray silently. Suddenly, Norman's face broke into a wide, joyful smile, and he raised his head as if turning toward the sun. Father Paul and I looked at each other in amazement and awe, wondering what we were witnessing, then turned our attention back to our patient.

Norman maintained the ecstatic smile for a full fifteen to twenty seconds. Then he relaxed his shoulders, let out a breath, and left his body, just as simply and quietly as that.

Norman's family arrived only minutes later. They were initially sad that they had not been present at the time of his death, but they were happy and grateful when they heard how extraordinary his passing had been. As his daughter expressed it, "Daddy finally got to see what he's been teaching all his life!"

Chapter 34

A Sister's Farewell

Georgia and Lilly had been more than sisters; they had been the best of friends. They had seen each other through the divorce of one spouse and the death of the other and had become constant companions. Pictures on the walls and tables showed two dynamic personalities that matched perfectly—posing in crazy hats in one picture, yakking it up at a party in another, clowning on a cruise ship in a third one. Georgia could not believe that she might lose her sister and told me she had no intention of doing so. With this in mind, when I saw Lilly for the first time, my heart just sank.

Here was a woman who was only a shadow of herself, skeleton-thin and wasted away, with not enough energy to turn herself over in bed. When she saw me, her thin face crumbled like a cookie and she started to cry. When her sister left the room for a moment, Lilly whispered, "I can't do this anymore. You have to help me tell her. She needs to know." I told Lilly that she didn't have to do anything anymore, squeezed her hand, and prepared for the conversation that would follow by asking God to give me the words to ease the blow.

Georgia came back into the room, and Lilly nodded at me and implored me with her eyes. I told Georgia exactly what Lilly had said. Lilly nodded with acknowledgment as I said the words that were coming from my heart: that she had fought the cancer longer than she desired because it meant so much to Georgia; that Lilly felt there was a much better place for her now, with God; that she didn't want to be sick in bed on earth. The words were divinely guided because I could see the relief and gratitude in Lilly's eyes as I spoke.

Georgia first appeared shocked; then she started to cry, and she cried for a long while. But before I left that day, she was able to tell Lilly that she understood and that her sister should go if she needed to. The relief on Lilly's face was a thing of beauty I will never forget.

When I came back the next day, Georgia told me that, just after my departure the day before, Lilly had smiled a huge smile and looked at the ceiling. This made Georgia happy because she hadn't seen her sister smile in weeks. She asked Lilly what she was looking at, and Lilly said, "I see the earth! I'm floating above the earth and it's *so* beautiful! I'm part of the universe!" She reached up with her thin, weak arms in longing for something that Georgia couldn't see but the presence of which she could feel. Lilly fell into a calm sleep a little while later, with the smile still on her face.

When Georgia finished the story, I explained that the dying are often able to see things that the rest of us can't, because the veil is thinner for those whose sprit is being called. Then I went in to see Lilly.

Within seconds of my entering the room, Lilly's breathing pattern began to change, becoming slower and shallower. I encouraged Georgia to sit on Lilly's bed so that she could be close to her sister. Georgia took Lilly's hand in her own and suddenly looked at me with a shocked expression. She said, "I can feel her leaving! I can feel her energy pulling away!"

At that second, Lilly died, peacefully and quietly, her soul simply freeing itself from the body that held it. Later, Georgia told me that she had seen, as had I, a "wisp, like smoke or fog" hover over Lilly's body in the moments after she died. Georgia was so grateful that she was given the opportunity to feel the awesome spiritual energies that were present in the moment of her sister's dying experience. She held in her heart the knowledge that this was meant as a special goodbye from the person she had loved the most.

Part Five

Tough Customers

We are ignorant of the Beyond because this ignorance is the condition of our own life, just as ice cannot know fire except by melting and vanishing.

—Jules Renard

Patients come in all ages, shapes, sizes, and temperaments. Of course, the meek and quiet ones are the easiest to get along with, are usually compliant with the care plan you set in place for them, and are good about following the suggestions of the medical staff who care for them. They present very few problems or challenges, and the visits with them are usually pleasant.

But I've said it before and I'll say it again: I'll take the spunky ones any day! Yes, they do give you a run for your money but, in many ways, they're a lot of fun. I had a diabetic patient who sat on, and smashed, his box of Fannie May candies, trying to hide the evidence while looking me straight in the eye and swearing he didn't know why his blood sugars were so high.

I had an oxygen-dependent patient who would open her bathroom window, even on the coldest day of winter, to stick her head out and smoke a cigarette that she was sure I wouldn't be able to detect on my next visit—or so she thought!

Another patient with severe lung disease called complaining of acute shortness of breath, only to admit that she had been hauling wheelbarrows of dirt around the backyard on a 90-degree day! These folks definitely were going to die the way they had lived, and I loved the spunk and spirit that had brought them this far in their lives. Like they say, you don't want to arrive at the end of your life with everything perfect and intact. You want to arrive with the wrinkles, bumps, and bruises of having had a darned good time!

These next stories are about patients of this type, whom I loved and respected for keeping their blustery, slightly intimidating, and unique personalities intact, even as their lives were coming to an end.

Chapter 35

Star Struck

Lorraine was in love with Bob Barker of *The Price is Right*. If I arrived at her home for my nursing visit while this show was on TV, she would make me sit in a corner until a commercial break, at which point she would frantically motion me over while she rolled up her sleeve to have her blood pressure taken. Once the show started again, I'd have to sit quietly until the next commercial, when I would hurry over to do another two-minute portion of my assessment. If I ran longer than the time of the commercial, Lorraine would wordlessly but sternly point to the chair in the corner, making me feel like a naughty school girl. At the end of an hour, I would have barely made any progress on the visit and would have been told to "Shush!" more times than I could count, because Lorraine's "beloved" was speaking on the TV.

Whereas some dying patients look forward to the day they will meet their Creator after their death, all Lorraine could talk about, as her eyes glazed over, was being face-to-face with—guess who? Her heartthrob, Bob Barker.

It is amazing to see how routinely some people carry on with their lives even though they have been told, and often know intuitively, that they don't have much time to live. Eventually, after the shock wears off, they go right back to their television shows, making curtains for the kitchen, or reading romance novels. Some of us believe that if we were the main character in that scenario, we might become paralyzed in our ability to move forward with routines or even to continue to pursue things that previously fed our passion. This does happen occasionally, but the majority of the people I have met in this situation pick themselves up, dust themselves off, and attempt to live the rest of their lives with little interruption, no matter the length. It may be a subdued version of their previous activities, due to the toll that illness usually takes on their bodies, but they move forward to continue living their lives, just the same.

I started to plan my visits to Lorraine for different times of the day, only to discover that she had taped the shows and would watch them one after another, pretty much all day long. This was obviously an inconvenience for me, but the reward of actually seeing stars in the eyes of an eighty-six-year-old after watching her Hollywood "crush" almost made it worth it. I became fairly efficient at doing short spurts of assessments while Lorraine was in my care. She never apologized for her behavior and never needed to: she was who she was.

Just as decisively, with no fanfare and in her no-nonsense fashion, Lorraine simply went to bed one night and passed away, never to see Bob Barker or me again. At least, not on earth.

Chapter 36

Letty, My British Import

Letty was a force to be reckoned with. Age eighty, height not quite up to my chin, and about the weight of a straw broom, she was nonetheless formidable and made up in will-power what she lacked in size. She had never married or had children; and she had moved all the way "across the pond" from England, and from her immediate family, many years ago. She shared her apartment with a cat, which I think must have been as intimidated by her as the rest of us were, because I never saw it once in the several months that I visited Letty.

Letty's nephew, Gavin, was the only relative who lived locally, and he had the unlucky honor of being named her power of attorney for healthcare and finances when Letty's health began to fail. If I hear that a "Saint Gavin" has been canonized, I'll know immediately who he is and why he was bestowed the honor. I would also give him my vote, in a heartbeat. I would frequently leave Letty's apartment with my confidence bruised from her brusque treatment, and I knew that Gavin spent much more time in her grumpy company than I did. I can still hear his calm, gentle voice, saying, "Now, Auntie . . . " as she blustered over some new issue or a perceived infraction of her rules.

CHAPTER 36

On my first visit to assess her condition, Letty scolded in her clipped British accent, "Sit straight or you'll grow crooked!" She was so intimidating in her countenance that I never even considered countering with the fact that I was finished with growing at age fifty!

On my second visit, she slapped my hand because she didn't like the blood pressure reading that I had taken. Slap! "Take it again!" she demanded. And a third time. Slap! I knew that if she heard a number she liked she'd probably tell me to write it on my report, but instead she gave up and announced, "Well, now you've gotten me all upset, so there's no point in taking it, is there?"

On yet another visit, she informed me that I use the word *okay* much too often to be polite and that this showed "a distinct lack of intelligence." At subsequent visits, she greeted me with, "Get on with it," or "You're a pokey one, aren't you?" I couldn't do anything right with Letty, or so it seemed.

Then, one day, out of the clear blue sky and for no apparent reason, she changed right in front of my eyes. It may have been the prayer I whispered each time I rang the doorbell, "Lord, please don't let her *bite* me," or, more often, "Lord, help me understand Letty." Letty began to smile, and she showed a twinkle in her eye that I never in my wildest dreams suspected had been hiding there. One day, she insisted that Gavin buy her a Polaroid camera; and, when she got it, she began demanding that each and every visitor have a picture taken with her. She learned to enlarge them on her computer to full-page photos, and then she would present the portraits to her visitors when they next returned. This was very unusual behavior for cantankerous Letty, who had historically never let herself be photographed. This new Letty smiled more often and began to relax and enjoy life. And I began to love her.

Poor Letty was in hospice with a diagnosis of COPD, a serious, chronic lung condition, and after several months she began to decline. I started to see that she no longer had the energy to insist, protest, or bulldoze her way through issues. More significantly, she stopped taking photographs. She became docile and weak, sleeping much of the time. At the end of one of our Friday visits, I said I would return on Monday to check on her. She started to weep, and she let me hold her hand for the first time.

Then she said, "I've been a bit of a grump. You've been awfully good to me and I love you dearly, but I won't be here on Monday. You see, I'm going to die tomorrow, Dear." I hugged her and, when she fell asleep, I quietly left.

True to Letty's stubborn British nature, she died the following day, quietly in her sleep. I keep the smiling portrait of my favorite little grump with the twinkle in her eye where I can look at it and remember her often.

Chapter 37

Late-Night Goodbye

When he first began receiving hospice services, Richard was still the independent, authoritative person he had been most of his life. He had served as a Navy pilot in World War II and, afterward, as a well-respected detective and as watch commander for the police force of a major city in the Midwest. He had many stories to tell, but he rarely spoke of them because he seemed to carry a lot of pain from the experiences he had had in both those roles. Occasionally, the "cop" in him would come out and he would deliver a line like, "Look me in the eye when you answer, because I've been trained to spot a lie in a second!" I was always on my best behavior with him and never risked the chance of being less than truthful, lest he recognize it.

Back in those days, when Richard was stronger, he took great joy in firing an unexpected question at a visitor, just for the enjoyment of watching the object of his query squirm. He directed this ploy at me on many occasions, only eventually to laugh at my discomfort and say, "It's okay, I was just kidding." I felt that he was trying to keep his old policeman skills sharp and having some fun in the process. Despite his brusque and sometimes crotchety manner, I rarely left a visit with him without his saying tenderly, "Stay safe," as I was leaving.

Over a period of three years, with Richard in and out of hospice with a diagnosis of Parkinson's disease, we saw this strong, decisive man become weaker and less and less able to control his surroundings, his business, and his own needs. To those of us who visited him, it was a sad situation, indeed, because he was aware of every minute detail of the decline in his condition. He was alternately angry, sad, remorseful, and bitter, but rarely accepting. This was the task of the hospice team: to help him gain acceptance and bring closure to his condition and his life.

Richard died suddenly, and our hospice team, who had grown so fond of the old curmudgeon, was not present at the time of his death. When I got a phone call early that day, informing me that he had died, I wept and felt a strong sense of loss all day.

That very night, I was on call and driving home after having just completed a visit to another patient. I turned a corner and saw that there were red and blue police lights behind my car. Confused, I stopped and thought, "*Now* what did I do?" A young police officer approached my window and shined his flashlight into my eyes. He said, "Hi! Why are you driving without your headlights on?"

Surprised, and seeing that he was right, I started to explain that I had stopped for gas and must have forgotten to turn them back on. But before I finished saying this, he fired back, "Where did you buy the gas?"

I was caught off-guard, as this was the last thing I expected him to ask. I stuttered, "Uh . . . back at the . . .

you know . . . the one with the carwash, uh . . . it's on the corner of . . . uh. . . ." And yes, I started to squirm!

The policeman suddenly and unexpectedly laughed and said, "It's okay, I was only kidding." He asked where I lived; and, still speechless, I pointed down the road. He said, "You just stay safe. And have a very good night." He tapped the car door twice with his knuckles, then smiled a huge smile and walked away. In his smile, I saw Richard's wonderful spirit and his last farewell to me.

Chapter 38

The Next Stop

I have my own firm beliefs regarding what happens to us when we die. We all know for a fact that the physical body stops living, but there are many, many beliefs about what else might happen. The beliefs seem to be separated into two main camps:

In one camp are the spiritual believers, who accept as true that our souls go to heaven or to another resting place; that our souls return as a spark to the flame which is God; or that our soul chooses another body with the purpose of returning to earth for another life in order to learn further lessons. In any case, the spiritual believers conclude that there is "another place" or a "better place" for the soul after death.

In the second camp are the people who do not believe that any type of spiritual existence follows this one. I have heard people express this school of thought by saying that, once the body dies, everything is over; or, if there is a soul, it dies with the body. I have even been told that after life there's nothing but "a big black hole."

As a hospice nurse, I feel it is not my right or my purpose to influence others with my thoughts or beliefs on any subject, particularly where spirituality or religion are concerned.

This boundary is an important one that I must always recognize and honor. It asks that I respect other people's beliefs, even if I don't agree with or understand them, and that I must never attempt to impose my own beliefs on them. This can be difficult at times. For instance, the "big black hole" that a patient, Dennis, expressed throughout his life as his belief about what happens when the body dies didn't look so friendly when he reached the precipice between life and death himself. He struggled greatly during his last days to find a comforting and honest answer to the new and urgent questions about death and dying that were brought to the surface as he faced his own mortality. When this happens, how I would love to share the simple but comforting beliefs of my own that allow me to be unafraid of death! Instead, I pray that a loving touch and a strong heart connection will do the job.

Here are more specific beliefs and ideas patients have shared with me regarding what happens after the physical body dies:

- "Nothing happens. We just turn into dust."
- "We go back to the Garden of Eden before the fall from Grace."
- "After our soul has returned to God for divine direction, we are born again, months or years later, to another body in which we have another opportunity to better ourselves and become more like God."
- "We go to purgatory, or to heaven if we're good, or to hell if we aren't. Forever."

- "We reincarnate as any living thing—even an insect or an animal—to understand that particular perspective of the universe."
- "We become stars in the universe."
- "We finally understand our place in creation and our connection to everything that is or ever has been."
- "There's nothing after this. When our body decays, we're gone forever."
- "Our soul remains as energy after our body dies."

One night, while on call, I attended the death of a man whose family I had not previously met. When I entered the small but cluttered home, I couldn't help but notice that the walls were covered with multiple posters of the planets and pictures taken by the Hubble Telescope. I saw a map of the galaxies, the God's Eye Nebula, the Milky Way, and the colorful gasses around Saturn. Magazines strewn about the room obviously belonged to someone who was very interested in stargazing.

I asked the deceased patient's wife how long her husband had been ill, and she told me that he had been diagnosed with lung cancer six years before. Understanding what a long road of illness he must have faced, I commented, comfortingly I thought, that it was a blessing that he was no longer sick and was now "in a better place."

She turned to me then, folded her hands in her lap, raised an eyebrow, and asked nicely but pointedly, "Oh, really. And where exactly *is* he?"

Feeling that my comment had been quite benign, as beliefs go, I was surprised by her question. I explained that, in my personal belief system, he had returned to God the Creator and to the home of our souls that we refer to as *heaven*. She looked at me with wide eyes, even disbelief, and commented, "WOW! Your answer is WAY out there!" My own curiosity now piqued, I asked where *she* thought her husband had gone. She readily replied, "Well, *of course*, he went to another galaxy!" I realized that, through my work in hospice, I had probably heard only a small sampling of the beliefs people hold about death and the afterlife.

During the remainder of this visit, while we waited for the funeral home personnel to arrive, I safely kept our topic of conversation to less controversial subjects.

Part Six

Comic Relief

Perhaps they are not stars but rather openings in heaven, where the love of our lost ones pours through and shines down upon us to let us know they are happy.

—Eskimo Proverb

"Hospice humor" may sound like an oxymoron, but believe me when I say that it is absolutely necessary and very much appreciated when it occurs. The job of hospice workers contains so much sadness, grieving, and loss that the flipside of the coin is always welcome. It comes unexpectedly, like the day I mentioned to a male patient that I was going to change his urinary catheter. With his permission, I pulled up his hospital gown, only to hear him mutter under his breath, "Oh, for heaven's sake! I don't know why they call 'em your 'privates'! As soon as you get sick, everyone looks at 'em! They oughta' call 'em your 'publics.'" I laughed so hard that I could hardly perform the intervention I had planned to do.

The next five stories illustrate other patients and families who were caught in the act of providing comic relief to a job where its appearance is rare.

Chapter 39

Too Much Information

Dollie was dying of lung cancer, and her family was taking care of her at home. Dollie's teenage daughters, Jan and Janie, had never experienced death so close to them and were doing their very best to provide care and compassion and meet the hands-on needs of their mother. They were assisted in these tasks by their stepdad, Danny. Danny was a truck driver and a little rough edged, but caring nonetheless. Danny, more than anyone, listened to the teaching of the hospice staff and took it to heart, wanting to do everything he could to make his wife comfortable and content.

Initially, when I first began to visit Dollie's apartment, she was staying alone during the day while her daughters went to school and Danny worked. In a very short time, it was clear that Dollie was no longer able to stay alone, as she was getting weaker and unable to meet her own needs. Regardless of the inconvenience, this is a safety concern. Especially given a patient's already compromised condition, one fall on the way to the bathroom or to the kitchen for a glass of water could result in a serious injury.

CHAPTER 39

At this time in a patient's illness, it is also prudent and advisable to have durable medical equipment, or DME, in the home to assist the patient in making daily life simpler and safer. The list is endless: grab bars for the shower, walkers, wheelchairs, hospital beds, over-the-bed tables, transfer devices, and bedside commodes are just the beginning of items that are available.

Another concern that medical personnel have when caring for a patient at home is that of insuring the safety of the caregiver, meaning the person who is providing personal care to the patient. Heavy lifting and patient transfers, or even frequent bending and stooping can put a caregiver at risk of injury. When the injury of a caregiver occurs, everyone involved is faced with a new problem: now who will care for the patient? Dollie, who had been adamantly independent up until now, agreed to have some of the DME items brought into her home. Once she got into the hospital bed, she began to decline, and it was clear that she was never going to get out of bed again.

Dollie had made several attempts to plan her own funeral. This is not unusual when certain patients have truly accepted the fact that their life is ending. As surprising as it is to others, there is a sense of comfort and closure for them to be able to have a say in the music, flowers, and clothing that will be part of the funeral. Dollie no longer had the strength to do the legwork, but she told Danny what she wanted and how she wanted it done. Weakly, she told him, "Don't forget my wig . . . and a push-up bra for the viewing in the casket." The wig she already had, but Jan and Janie rushed out to purchase the other requested item.

Danny made an appointment at the funeral home and came home pleased and relieved that he had been able to finalize most of the funeral plans to Dollie's specifications. In hushed whispers, he told me about "the beautiful casket—not the most expensive but not a cheapy, either"—and said that Dollie's body would be placed in a mausoleum where the remains of her other family members had been laid to rest. Because Dollie had wanted to be involved in the planning of her own funeral, I told Danny I thought it would be appropriate if he shared with her the plans that had been made.

Dollie was in a semicoma by this time but could be roused for short periods. I wasn't sure if she would respond to the information, but I encouraged Danny to tell her because it might give her peace of mind to know that her wishes had been carried out. Danny leaned over her bed and said, "Honey, it's all taken care of, just like you wanted." Dollie didn't respond, and Danny looked up at me. I nodded for him to go on. "I picked out the casket. You're really going to like it. It's the same color as the kitchen paneling in the trailer in Wisconsin. And, uh . . . the mausoleum? You're in a great spot—you're on the upper right-hand corner of the top shelf." Then, as if unable to stop himself from saying more, he blurted, "And honey? If you went straight diagonal down to the compartment on the left, you won't believe it: you're at your sister's!"

I wasn't sure if I should laugh or cry. But Dollie took care of the matter without my doing either. She opened one eye, looked at Danny, and whispered, "How much did all that cost?"

Chapter 40

Hospice and Hamsters

Death is part of life, and every person will eventually have to go through a death experience with a loved one. It is wonderful practice for children to witness death in nature and in other small ways that prepare them for the finality of losing someone they care about. We've all seen the elaborate funerals that children prepare for a dead toad they find in the garden, a baby bird that falls from a nest, or a family pet that dies of sickness or old age. Tiny crosses made of twigs and string, or rocks with "Fluffy" or other pet's names written in crayon, grace the backyards of most children.

My four-year-old granddaughter, Ramona, had a limited understanding of my work in hospice, but she knew that I "help people who are too sick to get better" and that sometimes I "help them get to heaven." Like most four-year-olds, she had no personal experience with death, but she knew that it was serious and permanent.

One morning, Ramona woke up to find that her two hamsters, Giraffey and Toto, had gotten into a fight. Giraffey was weak and bleeding, and my daughter felt that the little animal would most likely die from her injuries.

She explained the situation to tearful Ramona, telling her that "sometimes the people who love their pets have to help them die when they get hurt so that they don't suffer."

Ramona was quiet for a moment, considering this, then said solemnly, "Call my Grandma. She knows all about this."

To help Ramona with the anticipatory grieving of her little friend, I sat and talked to her about some of the loss of life that she had seen in her collection of Disney movies. She looked thoughtful for a moment and then quoting from her favorite one, *The Lion King*, she said, knowingly, "Oh, I get it. This is the 'circle of life.'"

Ramona felt happy that she had made the little animal comfortable with soft tissues on which to lie and a frequent whisper of, "It's okay; it's going to be alright." Giraffey lived another day and then died as expected. To assist the grieving process, Ramona buried her friend in a colorful box under a lilac bush. With just a little bit of teaching, this four-year-old was able to face her first real loss with acceptance, along with her little-girl tears.

Chapter 41

A New Intervention

In hospice, as patients become weaker and are unable to swallow efficiently, we often resort to other ways of giving medications. One method is to use a transdermal patch, which allows medication to be absorbed through the skin. Another is the sublingual method. This involves using a small dropper to administer tiny amounts of liquid medication, which is about the consistency of maple syrup, under the tongue or in the cheek pocket. The medication goes directly into the bloodstream from the mouth tissues, eliminating the need for the patient to have to swallow pills. These methods of medication administration are a godsend, making it certain that symptoms of pain, anxiety, congestion, and labored breathing can be managed well into the dying process when a person becomes weak or even unconscious. Often our pharmacist will flavor the sublingual medications to make them more palatable, as the natural flavors can be bitter or unpleasant. Spearmint is the most common flavor used. Once the nurse explains the directions for the administration of these medications, family members become adept at recognizing signs and symptoms and are able to use these medications to provide comfort to their loved one.

Jackie was dying of liver cancer and began to require use of these sublingual medications for pain and anxiety. She tried, and spit out, every flavor we could find: mint, raspberry, orange, chocolate, you name it. She would spit and say, "I can *still* taste the medicine!" One evening as she was falling into a fitful sleep, her twin grown daughters, Sue and Sarah, decided to sneak her a dose, hoping to make her more comfortable. Remembering what they had been told about the medicine being able to work through the oral tissues and go directly into the bloodstream, they conferred and decided to try a different route.

They met me at the door the next morning for my scheduled visit and disclosed what they felt was a breakthrough route of administration for the medication. Proudly they relayed that, when Jackie had fallen into a restless sleep the night before, they had tiptoed quietly into the room and dispensed the medication—using her belly button as the receptacle for the morphine!

Knowing that some teaching was in order, and not wanting them to feel that they had done something that I found hilarious rather than ingenious, I asked them how Jackie had slept during the night.

"Great!" they said, "She never woke up once!"

I was concerned that Jackie had technically not had any pain medication since my last visit and might have experienced discomfort. Still trying to hide my amusement at their route of administration, I asked the daughters how Jackie had felt when she woke up that morning.

Without missing a beat, they looked at each other and said, "Sticky!"

Chapter 42

Did They Really Say That?

Over the years, I have heard hilarious comments and ideas from hospice patients, even as they are getting ready to abandon their earthly bodies. The following are pearls of wisdom, taken from real conversations with them.

- I was sitting on a loveseat next to a hundred-year-old man, taking his blood pressure:

  ME: "Mr. Jones, your blood pressure is a little bit high today."
  MR. JONES (blushing): "That's because I have my hand on your knee."

- I was assessing a patient's comfort level:

  ME: "Elsie, do you have any pain?"
  ELSIE: "Well, only when it hurts."

- A female patient told me that she would like to have a small, ticking clock with her when she was buried.

ME: "Why do you need a clock with you, Ethel?"
ETHEL: "So I have something to listen to until I get used to being dead."

Sometimes patients think that, just because we're experts on dying, we're also experts on heaven. These innocent questions were asked by patients during our discussions of dying:

- "Do you know how many light years it takes to get to heaven?"
- "Nurse, I'm not as strong as I used to be. Do you know how much my wings will weigh?"
- "In heaven, can we wear any color we want? I don't look good in white."

Sometimes questions come out of the blue:

- PATIENT: "Is there a special test you have to take to work in hospice?"

  ME: "Do you mean . . . like a nursing board exam?"
  PATIENT: "No, I mean like a 'niceness' test."

- As I arrived in the early morning at a patient's home dressed in colorful scrubs, she looked surprised and asked, "Why did you come in your pajamas? Did you get up late?"
- I asked a frail and tired hundred-and-four-year-old patient if she had any idea why she had lived so long, and she answered, "I don't know . . . but don't do it!"

- After an elderly gentleman had had several setbacks in his health, he looked at me and said morosely, "Let me tell ya,' getting old ain't for sissies."
- One of my patient's advance directives included her wishes "to be waked in my pink bathrobe, with the TV remote in one hand and a picture of Elvis Presley in the other." (And, yes, she was.)

Sometimes it's the situation, and not the words that make it funny:

- I taught the daughters of one patient to use small sponges on sticks, called mouth swabs, to provide moisture to their father's mouth after he was unable to drink fluids. I found out several days later that, at his request, they were swabbing his mouth with Jack Daniels.
- I was helping a man make cremation plans for his wife and discussing the receptacle that would be used to hold her ashes. Throughout the whole conversation, no matter how many times I corrected him, he consistently called the *urn* a *urinal*. "How many days after the cremation does it take to get my wife back in the urinal?" (Oh, the mental picture this creates!)
- A patient and her family wanted to give me a boost when I was experiencing a busy and trying time. As a surprise, when I arrived at their home, the patient was dressed as the caregiver, the caregiver was dressed as the patient, and the patient's daughter was dressed

as the visiting home-care physician, right down to the striped tie, blue lab coat, and clipboard!

- One dying patient, a would-be comedian, used every opportunity he could find to insert the word *dead* into our conversations. He became an expert at it:

  If I made a noise in the room, he said, "You'll wake the dead."
  If I said something he disagreed with, he remarked, "I think you're dead wrong."
  When I left his home, he cautioned, "Don't forget to deadbolt the door."
  If he was in disagreement on a part of his care plan, he would say we were "deadlocked" on the issue.
  Because he had been ill for a long time and was tired of the limitations that his illness imposed, he said that, when his time finally came, he would be the "Grateful Dead."

Chapter 43

Brave Dave

When I was told that my new patient was a twenty-seven-year-old man with end-stage malignant melanoma, I wondered how I would ever manage this case emotionally. This patient was only a few years older than my son, and that felt too close for comfort. Once I met David, though, I relaxed. I relaxed because *he* was relaxed, yet I didn't understand how this could be. Even at my own age, I was not ready to break my stride or hand my life over to death. How could someone at his young age be ready?

David met me at the door with a handshake and a smile. He had the greenest eyes I have ever seen. One brief glance told me that he was a very sick young man. He was completely bald, and his skin was the color and texture of grey car upholstery, indicating the seriousness of his condition. David told me that he had been diagnosed only three weeks earlier with malignant melanoma. He added that he had felt unwell for many months before then but had chosen to ignore his symptoms. His disease by that time was so advanced that he had been told he had only a week or so to live. He had moved back home to be cared for by his parents and younger siblings.

"A week isn't very long," he said, "But it's long enough to plan my funeral." I marveled at how comfortably David talked about the fast-approaching end to his life. What was most amazing was seeing how he was comforting others in their grieving about his own impending death. More than once, I saw him hug his mother and father and ask gently, "Are you doing okay?"

When I came to visit, David would show me the contents of a notebook he was keeping to plan his funeral. On one page was the list of pallbearers he had chosen: his brothers and special friends. On another page were the songs that he wanted played at his wake: songs by Queen and Aerosmith and Journey. And on another page he had listed who would receive the things he was leaving behind, everything from his underwear to his car! To see this young man, whose life had barely begun, attain such peace and acceptance of his ever-nearing death was awe inspiring.

The last time I saw David, just before he died, he turned to me and said, "I'm so grateful for hospice. I'd be willing to do a commercial for you." In typical David-style, he turned as if facing the camera, smiled, and said, "Use hospice. They make dying a pleasure."

Part Seven

Cultural Differences

All changes, even the most longed for, have their melancholy, for what we leave behind us is a part of ourselves. We must die to one life before we enter into another.

—Anatole France

Any walk of life that takes one into the private lives and homes of other people can, and certainly will, show you a more vast variety of living styles and family dynamics than you ever thought possible. Whether this assortment of styles exemplifies cultural, social, educational, or economic differences, it will, without a doubt, humble the ethnocentric streak in any of us.

Believing that "our" way is the only way to think, live, or act doesn't hold much water when one steps into a world unlike one's own. What is considered the "norm" to one person may be beyond comprehension to another, depending on one's socialization and previous experience. For me, this has always been a fascinating aspect of my role as an RN case manager. The next few stories will give just a slice of the types of differences that might be experienced in a day in the life of a hospice nurse.

Chapter 44

An Indian Princess

I was on call and was asked to go to the death of a young Indian woman who had died of breast cancer. I knew from the report of the triage nurse that she had a husband and one child, a twelve-year-old son, so I was unprepared when I walked up the front steps of the luxurious home and saw no less than a hundred pairs of shoes beside the porch. I slipped off my own shoes, knowing that, in this house, it was customary to do so, and then knocked on the door. It was opened by a middle-aged East Indian man who said nothing but indicated with his hand for me to follow him into the next room. As I turned the corner of the foyer, I encountered close to a hundred people, men on one side of the room, and women on the other. They filled the large living room, the kitchen, and the stairway. You could have heard a pin drop in the silence, and every eye was on me. I saw a man and a boy standing next to the hospital bed in the center of the living room. I approached and asked if they were Shakti's husband and son. They nodded. I asked if Shakti's death had been peaceful.

Her husband, Paben, looked at me with big eyes and replied in broken English, "I do not know. We are not certain that she has died." I patted his shoulder and walked to the bedside. In the bed was the most beautiful woman I had ever seen. Every feature was perfect and delicate, like a child's. Even in death, she was stunningly beautiful.

I think it was denial that made her husband say he wasn't sure if Shakti had died. She was obviously no longer breathing, and the color was beginning to fade from her velvety skin. As is the custom when I am pronouncing a patient's death, I put my stethoscope to her chest and listened, although I knew that no heartbeat remained. After half a minute, I turned to Paben and said quietly, "Your wife has died, Paben."

Immediately the room, which had been as quiet as if it had been empty, erupted in sound. The women on one side of the room began to wail and moan and hug each other fiercely and randomly. The men on the other side of the room were huddled in groups, chattering loudly, and gesturing with their hands. I had no idea where to begin to comfort this large crowd of people. My instinct told me just to quietly observe and wait a while. After a few minutes, I could see that the way Shakti's family and friends were grieving was traditional and natural for them.

A short while later, I explained to Paben that I would need to make a number of official phone calls, as is the protocol when there is a home death. I then asked him if he would like me to bathe and dress his wife's body before she was taken to the funeral home. He smiled gratefully and left the room to gather clothes and bathing supplies. At that moment, two women, one who was Shakti's friend and the other who was her sister, approached me and said quietly, "We will assist you."

Paben arrived with the gathered items and made a short announcement to the other people. In an instant, the room was empty except for beautiful Shakti, her sister, her friend, and me. My assistants encouraged me to do the washing, and they followed two steps away, one holding a stack of clean linens and the other holding an elaborately painted bowl with scented water. We carefully and lovingly bathed Shakti's body and rubbed her with oils.

Shakti had lost her hair during chemotherapy treatments over the past several months, and it had just begun to grow back. Although her hair was as soft as bird feathers, it was very short and uneven, creating a distinct contrast to her exotic Indian features. Her sister carried forward a box; when she opened it, I saw a luxurious, shiny, black wig for Shakti to wear. I eased it over her head and smoothed and fluffed it. She was beautiful! Shakti's friend brought two more boxes to the bed. Inside the larger box was the most exquisite red garment I had ever seen. It was trimmed with gold and as diaphanous as a spider's web. We eased Shakti's body into loose-fitting trousers and a midriff blouse and wrapped the yards of fabric that made up her sari around her. The smaller box was then opened, and the two women proceeded to place every piece of gold jewelry that the box held onto Shakti. Six necklaces, a dozen bracelets, earrings, several rings, and an elaborate bindi for the center of her forehead were all carefully put into place. I stood back and looked at Shakti; she was transformed.

Lying in the bed was a foreign Indian princess, like the ones they show in children's fairy tales. I could see how she must have looked at a party or on her wedding day.

I could see how proud her husband must have been of his wife. I could see why one hundred people had come together tonight. She took my breath away.

Paben and the mass of people returned to the room; and they stood, I believe, in as much awe as I at the beauty before us.

Within minutes, the funeral director arrived to take Shakti's body. An anxious Paben approached me and asked quietly if the whole group could follow the hearse to the funeral home. Quickly, I calculated the number of vehicles it would take to accomplish this and also noted the time on my watch: 2:45 a.m. Knowing the answer to my question, but asking out of respect for Paben, I told the funeral director what Paben had requested.

For only a split second, the director looked distraught at the idea. He then turned to Shakti's grieving husband and, placing his hand on Paben's shoulder, gently explained that there was no room for all these people at the funeral home, but that he would care for Shakti's body as if she were part of his own family. Paben was satisfied and comforted by this answer and nodded.

I assisted the funeral director in transferring Shakti's body to a gurney, and we carefully covered her with the cart's maroon velvet blanket. As he pushed the gurney toward the door, first all the men and then all the women lined up four abreast and followed the gurney to the waiting vehicle, chanting prayers all the way to the street. I, alone, stood in the doorway of the small mansion, watching the funeral procession of the princess.

Chapter 45

Hospice and S.W.A.T.

The admission paperwork instructed, "Knock at the front door, then let yourself in. Go straight down the hallway to the back bedroom, where you will find the patient, Beth." Hmmm. I knew from reading the previous report that Beth was a fifty-seven-year-old bedridden patient with multiple sclerosis, and I thought it highly unlikely that she would be living alone. When I arrived at her home, the first thing I noticed was that it was rundown, with a broken front door, torn screens, peeling brown paint, and overgrown weeds. This was in sharp contrast to the other homes around it, but I knew that Beth's long-term illness of MS would not have allowed her the physical strength it takes to maintain a home. I knocked at the front door and waited. Surely someone was here with her. When no one answered after the second knock, I turned the knob and went inside.

In what appeared to be the living room, the drapes and shades were drawn, creating a dim interior. The unpleasant smell of stale, stagnant air invaded the space. Until I was almost past them, I didn't see the sprawling figures of two young men sleeping on the adjacent couches.

Neither moved as I walked past, proceeding down the hall to Beth's bedroom.

She lay in the hospital bed, painfully thin, with the muscles of her legs contracted into what looked like a pretzel shape. Her bed linens were grey and rumpled, and piles of dirty laundry were in every corner of the room. Her unwashed hair was pulled up into a thin, tight ponytail on the top of her head, and her mouth was set in a scowl. "I'm *fine*," she said. "I don't *need* help. I don't *want* help. My son looks after me." Gently, I explained that hospice would be available for all the things she could no longer do: bathe herself, change her sheets, and straighten her room. It would even cover the cost of medication and medical equipment to make her more comfortable.

Beth wasn't happy and avoided looking at me, but the scowl had left her face. I performed a full assessment with her reluctant permission and then gently turned her over to check her back. There on her sacrum was a gaping hole—a bedsore the width of my hand—covered with a dirty dressing. As I cleaned the wound and changed the dressing, I noted how painful this was for Beth and immediately called her doctor to get an order of morphine. After a single small dose, Beth was pain free and completely relaxed. She began to tell me which television shows she liked to watch. She shared that her son worked nights and that he slept most of the day. I made a mental note that, if this was the case, how little time he had to spend actually caring for his mother. I left the bottle of morphine at her bedside and explained how much and how often to take the medication. After changing the bed sheets and tidying her room a little, I walked back through the house to the front door. I passed the two young men, neither of whom had moved an inch since I had come through the door over ninety minutes ago, and quietly let myself out.

Three days later, I arrived for my second visit. Again, but intentionally less quietly this time, I made my way past the two sleeping figures on the couch. Oh, wait, this time there were three, with one body sprawled on the floor. When I got to Beth's doorway, she immediately blurted out, "I need more morphine. I had a lot of pain. I used it all up. It really helps." This raised a red flag. She had used a whole bottle of morphine in three days? She insisted that, yes, she had taken a dose every two hours, which I had told her was the maximum frequency allowed with the order from her doctor because her pain was so bad.

I called the pharmacy and ordered a second bottle of morphine. As I hung up the phone, I turned to see a disheveled man about twenty-one years old standing in the doorway.

He glanced past me, not saying hello, and asked, "Mom, did you tell her you need more morphine?"

When Beth answered "yes," he walked out the doorway and back down the hall without another word. I asked Beth if that was her son, and she became immediately defensive.

"Yes," she said, "He takes good care of me." If I even attempted to get close to the subject of her son during the rest of the visit, I got an icy, cold stare from Beth. I noted on my way out of the house that Beth's son had assumed on the couch the position I had seen him in earlier, fast asleep.

CHAPTER 45

At this time, I called my manager and told her that I had growing concerns about Beth. These included, of course, the heavy use of her medication, but also that fact that she did not appear to be receiving the care she needed from her family, however firmly she argued otherwise. My manager told me that she would set up a care-plan conference with the hospice team and administration staff in two days' time.

One day later, I received a call from the hospice nursing assistant, Jill, who now reported, "I just gave Beth a bed bath and I'm leaving her home. She said to tell you that she needs more morphine." It was impossible that Beth was in that much pain. Also, according to Jill, none of Beth's needs had been met when Jill arrived. Beth had been hungry, thirsty, and unclean. I called Mary, the hospice social worker, gave her a summary of my concerns, and asked her to meet me at Beth's home.

Again, when I arrived at Beth's home, no one answered my knock. Again, two figures were asleep on the couch in the living room. After greeting Beth gently, I started my physical assessment of her and was trying to think of a way to broach the subject of the morphine and of the care that her son was—or wasn't—providing. Out of the corner of my eye, in a window to the right, I saw movement, but when I looked up, it was gone. A few minutes later, through another window, I saw it again. Then I could see a man in a dark suit and long coat walking toward the house over the backyard lawn. As I was easing Beth's clean hospital gown over her head, I heard BAM! BAM! Both the front and back doors flew open—actually, they were *kicked* open—at the same time. In both doorways, which I could see from the center of Beth's bedroom, stood men in dark suits and long coats and with guns in their hands. I heard scrambling noises coming from another area of the house, and the men ran in the direction of the sound. Beth and I remained where we were, terrified, until one of the men came into the room, showed me his detective's badge, and asked me to follow him into the living room.

They had raised the shades and opened the curtains. For the first time I could clearly see the mess and the people who were there. Beth's son and another young man were handcuffed and being searched by the detectives. The coffee table was strewn with prescription bottles of methadone, speed, drug paraphernalia—and the two empty bottles of Beth's morphine. The detectives left with the two men in custody.

When the social worker arrived a few minutes later, we calmed Beth as best we could and made arrangements for her to be admitted to a nursing home that same afternoon. She told me, before the ambulance came to transport her to her new home, that none of the morphine I had ordered had been given to her. Beth was kept comfortable in the nursing home, with medication and with hospice care, until she died several months later. She never saw her son again.

I believe that Beth would have suffered in silence and in isolation until she died, if God hadn't opened a window of opportunity for us to help her live her final months in peace and comfort.

Chapter 46

Caves and Cockroaches

Hospice or home-health personnel have to learn to fly by the seat of their pants sometimes, such as when a new patient is admitted, when new family members come into the picture, or when we make an on-call visit to a home we've never been to before. All these scenarios can, at times, feel intimidating and uncertain. Although we are trained to diffuse situations and people, sometimes what is required can be more than we can or should attempt. We are never required to enter or stay in a place where we feel unsafe, and for this reason we occasionally have to leave a home before we have completed our visit.

Examples include a patient's unstable daughter, who had previously been a Chicago police officer and still owned a gun; a patient or family member who was a known drug offender and obviously under the influence during staff visits; large, fierce dogs on the premises; and a multitude of other potential threats. In one circumstance, it was necessary for our hospice staff to have a police escort for every visit to a patient's home, due to the volatility of a family member. Experience and discernment play an important role in determining the safety of our staff as they enter a home.

On one particular morning, a student nurse was to meet me at the office for the purpose of "shadowing" me for several weeks to learn more about the areas of home health and hospice in her curriculum of nursing classes. Before we went on our rounds for the day, I had planned to spend an hour with her in the office explaining hospice philosophy and giving her a background report on the patients we would be visiting that day. However, the minute I arrived at the office, my pager sounded with the report of the death of a new patient, and I was being asked to attend. My antennas went up when further details on the report cautioned me that the patient's son was her primary caregiver and that he was mentally handicapped.

I weighed the decision of whether to take the student with me or to leave her at the office for another visit. I decided to let her make the choice. We hadn't even met yet; I had no idea about her personality or her comfort level in this situation. I knocked on the door of the meeting room where the students were receiving training from their nursing instructor. When I opened the door, a dozen faces looked back at me. "Lynda?" I asked. Abruptly, a tall, blonde, self-assured young woman smiled and stood, strode toward me, and stuck out her hand. I immediately sensed that she would have an adventurous attitude toward the situation we were facing. I told her about the visit I was about to make, giving her the option of staying behind if she chose to do so. Without hesitation, Lynda gathered up her belongings and said, "Let's go!"

It was only a short drive to the patient's home, and I hurriedly explained to Lynda what the hospice nurse's responsibilities are when we respond to the call of a death. Initially, we support the family in whatever way they need. Some families are unprepared, frantic and crying because their loved one has passed. Others are prepared and grieving calmly and quietly and want to tell us all about the deceased, bringing out photos and records of accomplishments. Some families want as much time as possible to hold their loved one's hand before he or she is taken from the home, and other families want the funeral director to come as quickly as possible. In some homes, there are young children, and it is appropriate and necessary to have a social worker present to meet their specific needs. Family members can be working well together to make final plans or decisions, or they can be embroiled in a power struggle about how things should get done. There can be long periods of waiting while distant family members make the drive to the home, or we might wait for a minister or priest to arrive for a special prayer or ceremony. All such above circumstances are sifted out piece by piece once we arrive in the home, and great care is taken to meet every need of every single person at this very emotional time.

After the initial assessment of what is needed and support to the family has begun, the hospice nurse officially pronounces the patient dead by checking for vital signs. When none are found—no heartbeat, no breathing—the time is noted and the official phone call to the coroner is made to report the death. Next comes the phone call to the funeral home, the doctor, and other hospice staff. At a death visit, I always offer to bathe and dress the deceased's body according to the family's wishes, and this is usually an offer they accept gratefully and graciously. Usually, the clean clothes they choose are mom's favorite nightgown or dad's favorite flannel pajamas. But I have also been asked to French-braid Grandma's hair, dress Joe in his golf clothes with a putter in his right hand and a picture of his wife in his pocket, or put Aunt Thelma's square-dancing dress on her because that's what she liked best.

For me, the offer I make is all about dignity, because no one should leave their home for the last time in a soiled diaper or a stained undershirt, or even something as generic as a hospital gown. I know that their soul will meet God shining and beautiful with no help from me, but I feel that their personal human "vehicle" should be meticulously clean when they leave.

Usually while waiting for the arrival of the funeral director, the nurse destroys leftover medications by detoxifying them in the kitty litter or coffee grounds she carries in her car. When the funeral director arrives, the nurse also helps transport the body onto the gurney and provides further support to the family, because this final moment—as their loved one leaves the home for the very last time—is difficult and sometimes traumatic, especially with the death of a child.

Lynda confessed to me, while I was giving her as much preparation for our visit as possible, that she had never seen or touched a deceased body before and that she had some trepidation about this first experience. I asked her to let me know if she was uncomfortable with anything once we got inside the house, and I would offer her the option of waiting for me in the car if necessary.

CHAPTER 46

We arrived at a ramshackle home with overgrown shrubs and old newspapers strewn about. All the doors and windows were shuttered tight despite the warm June weather. The doorbell was hanging by a wire, so reaching through the torn screen, I knocked at the door. A few seconds later, it was slowly opened by a very tall and disheveled man. I said gently, "Thomas? I'm Janet from hospice, and this is Lynda. I was told that your mother has just passed away. I'm here to help you." Without hesitation, without a word, he stood back to let us in.

From the tiny foyer, I could see the dining and kitchen area to the left and a hallway with what was probably the living area to the right. Although it was nearly nine o'clock in the morning, the house was as dim as a cave inside. Every window was covered with a heavy shade as well as a dark curtain, and all were pulled tightly shut. Every corner was filled with shadows and, as I had just come in from a sunny day, my eyes were having difficulty adjusting to the oppressive gloom. Thomas pointed down the hallway to the right and, with a heavy speech impediment, said, "My mom is in there." Then he motioned to the shadowy kitchen and said, "And I'm going in there." Thomas lumbered away, and Lynda and I moved down the hallway toward the living room.

In the duskiness, I saw a dark couch against the opposite wall. Two legs with shoes on the feet were visible in front of the couch. At first I thought, "Oh, my goodness. She died sitting up on the couch." But as Lynda and I got closer, I could see that the legs were attached to nothing. There wasn't a body there, just legs. Did the image of an ax murderer come to mind? I have to confess that it did. But, on further examination, I saw that these were two prosthetic limbs that had been propped up against the couch. I turned to look at Lynda's face and almost laughed out loud as I saw her mentally arriving at the same mistaken conclusion I had almost come to. "This patient was a double amputee, Lynda. Those are her prostheses," I whispered, and watched as relief flooded her face.

On the far right side of the room was the hospital bed, and in it lay Hazel's body. She looked elfin because she was already old and shrunken, but the fact that her legs ended at her knees made her look even more diminutive and fairy-tale like. I checked Lynda to assess her comfort level and saw her face soften. She reached down and touched Hazel's hand and then her face. Then she looked at me with wonder and said, "Wow. There's nothing scary about it, is there? Once we've died, it's just like an "Earthling suit" we leave behind; it's like our soul just unzips it, shrugs it off, and leaves."

I pondered Lynda's very articulate words, and we began to undress and bathe Hazel's body together. At my request, Thomas brought in clean clothes and underclothes, and Lynda and I provided Hazel with the dignity she so deserved when she left her home for the final time.

When we finished preparing Hazel for the arrival of the funeral director, I requested that Thomas sit and talk with us. I wanted to assess his emotional ability to deal with the death of his mother and to find out any funeral arrangements he may have made. Thomas wasn't about to share his intimate feelings with a stranger, if he had them, but he agreed to sit down to give us the other information we needed. I sat in a stiff wooden chair, and Lynda sat next to Thomas on the couch. I asked Thomas a question and looked up to see his face as he responded.

In the dimness of the room, I noticed the rapid movement of something on the couch behind him. First here, then there. In the next few seconds, literally dozens of cockroaches had come out from amidst the fabric of the couch where Thomas and Lynda were sitting. Thomas was unfazed, and Lynda was clueless. I quickly picked up my nursing bag and my folder from where I had placed them on the floor and pulled my feet up onto the lower supports of the chair. "Lynda," I said, "Bring your notepad and purse over here and sit next to me."

She smiled and leaned back—right against the back of the roach-infested couch—and said, "I'm okay. I'm comfortable here." A little louder, and in a little more forceful tone, I said, "You need to sit right *here*. Next to me. You need to be able to see what I'm doing." Reluctantly, Lynda moved over to the wooden chair beside me, and we completed our visit. Lynda looked at me curiously; she still had no idea why I was so insistent about her sitting beside me. Seconds later, the funeral director arrived and transported Hazel's body from the house. I told Thomas that a social worker would be along to see what she could do to help him, and he nodded.

Lynda and I said our goodbyes to Thomas at the door and got into the car. I turned the corner, out of Thomas's sight, and announced, "Everyone out of the car!" Lynda looked at me incredulously as I jumped out, kicked my shoes off, and dumped my entire nursing bag out onto the grass. All I could think of was the old adage that if you bring home one cockroach, you bring home hundreds. When I explained to Lynda what I was doing, she squealed and did the same. I've often wondered what conclusion neighbors may have come to as they saw two nurses shrieking and doing the heebie-jeebie dance on the corner that day.

Lynda and I spent the rest of our day making routine hospice visits, and she both enjoyed and benefited from what she learned. But I'm sure that the "baptism by fire" that she experienced during our first visit together that day stayed in her memory for a long time.

Chapter 47

Fatimah's Gift

I had just received the report on a new patient. She was fifty-two years old, the same age I was at the time, and was being admitted to hospice with a diagnosis of terminal ovarian cancer. I learned that she was married, had two college-age sons, and was from Afghanistan.

When the front door opened to my knock for my initial visit, a small, dark, beautiful woman motioned me inside. She had a shy smile and a gracious manner; and, when I introduced myself, she formally shook my hand and stated, "No one calls me Fatimah. Call me Solie."

Each time I visited Solie, she was alone. After my assessment and the medical part of our visit was finished, Solie wanted to know about my life. Usually I don't share personal information with clients because of my strict "it's not about me" policy. But Solie would gently urge me to tell her about myself. I eventually told her that I had been divorced and was newly engaged to be married again and that I had three grown children. She, in turn, told me about her husband, who was the love of her life, and about her two sons, of whom he was very proud. Over time, we had many discussions about marriage and motherhood, which Solie usually initiated.

During the second month of providing care for Solie, I arrived at her home to find several cars in the driveway. This was very unusual. When I entered the front door, both of Solie's sons and her husband, Bijan, were seated formally in the living room. They were dressed in button-down shirts and ties and appeared to be going to some formal event. Throughout the visit, Bijan seemed especially solicitous, carrying into the room plates of cookies and cups of tea and standing at my elbow as if ready to be of assistance, should I need anything. Their sons made little conversation, and I wondered what that meant. An Afghan custom, perhaps?

It was the middle of winter, and I had taken my shoes off at the front door so that I wouldn't track mud or snow into the house. As I was leaving and went to step back into my shoes, I noticed that they had been highly polished, shining on every surface. Was I imagining this?

On the next visit, Solie's sons were nowhere to be seen, but Bijan greeted me at the door. This time, when my visit was completed and I was able to slide my feet into my shoes, I found that, not only were they shined, but each held a shiny red apple and orange. What was this about?

I noticed now that Bijan was always home when I visited, and I concluded that he was staying home more because Solie was sicker and needing more help. But on the following visit, besides finding shiny shoes as I was leaving, I found a whole bag of fresh fruit beside them. And when I left the house, Bijan was at my side, with his arm looped through mine, assisting me down the icy driveway to my car. I was beginning to feel slightly uncomfortable with this unusual attention and decided to speak with Solie about it the next time we met.

Solie and I once again completed the medical portion of our visit; just as I was about to bring up my questions and concerns about my shoes, the fruit, and Bijan's attention, Solie handed me two wrapped gifts. Taken by surprise, I raised my eyebrows and asked, "Solie, what are these for?"

Solie replied, "These are gifts for you, my sister. Open them." The first gift was a small ceramic cottage. The roof lifted off, and Solie told me that it was for storing tea. We had shared many cups of tea together over the past several months, so she knew that this was something that I would use and treasure. The second gift was a bottle of cologne. I immediately noticed the name of the scent on the label, which read *Bijan*. "It's my favorite," Solie said as she smiled shyly.

I have been given many small gifts from patients over my years in hospice, but never something like this. My mind was racing, and my heart was sinking, as I thanked Solie and wondered what it all meant. I was soon to find out.

When I visited the next time, Solie was confined to bed and weak and restless. She held tightly to my hand and again called me "sister." She was painfully thin now, and I knew that she didn't have long to live. "Sister," she said, "I want to give you my husband." I started to protest, but she continued in her frail voice. "I know you are engaged, but Bijan is a good man. We've talked about it, and I told him that I picked you."

I struggled to find something comforting and peaceful to say to this woman who was ready to pass on her most valuable treasure to me. I knew I couldn't lie to her. "Solie," I said, "Sister, I can't marry Bijan, but I promise I'll make sure that he's okay after you're gone." I know she was disappointed, but she nodded and gave me a small, sad smile.

Solie died the next day, during my visit. She was peaceful at the time of her death, so I felt that she had accepted my decision. As promised, I made sure that a bereavement volunteer was assigned to help Bijan and his sons through the difficult months ahead.

Bijan made one more attempt, several months later, to see if Solie's plan might yet be feasible. He sent me a letter inviting my children and me to join him and his sons for dinner. I graciously declined, knowing that my "sister" would understand.

Part Eight

Closing Thoughts

A Friend for Me

Two little girls, one curly, one straight.
One bubbly, one shy. One blue-eyed, one brown.
Each intrigued with the other,
Crisp white blouses under plaid school uniforms,
Brand new tights on their skinny legs.
They met on the playground one sunny day,
Watching each other try their hand at hopscotch,
Chinese jump rope, chasing boys.
Soon they were giggling teens,
Sharing secrets of hair things and make-up,
Of heartbreaks and love,
Of dreams and uncertainty.
In the blink of an eye, they were new mommies together.
"Bottle or breast?" "Pacifier or thumb?"
"To scold, or to spank a little bottom?"
Without each other knowing, they plan:
"I will become a nurse!" And they did!
One welcoming tiny new souls into this world,
The other ushering tired souls Home.
Sharing the intimacies of the job in phone calls and letters:
"This patient." "That coworker." "Twelve-hour shifts."
Finding deeper questions to the meaning of life
By watching others live theirs.
Empty nests; their birdies have flown.

Now, into the twilight of a long friendship
That has endured almost half a century:
Could it be??
Holding the hand of my friend as she leaves,
Someone I've known almost as long as I've known myself.
Knowing that love goes on.

—Janet Wehr, in honor of my dear friend,
Karen Felcher, 1952–2009

My Personal Journey

Live for something—do good. And leave behind a monument of virtue that the storms of time can never destroy. Write your name in kindness, love, and mercy on the hearts of thousands you will come in contact with year by year, and you will never be forgotten. Your name and good deeds will shine as the stars of heaven.

—Thomas Chalmers

There is another factor that keeps me working with the dying, and it is a purely selfish motivator in my choice to continue to do this work. With my introduction to hospice care so many years ago, I was surprised to learn that I was discovering insights into myself that might have remained hidden and untapped had it not been for the introspection provided by the people I was meeting and the work I was doing.

Remember that, for nearly every patient I meet in hospice, tomorrow never comes. The diagnosis these people have been given is really a life sentence, and they are forced to face what most of us don't need or want to spend time speculating: How long do I have? What day will I die?

In delivering end-of-life care to others, I feel that I have been given an opportunity to live my own life differently than I might otherwise have. George Bailey, in the classic movie, *It's a Wonderful Life*, is given the chance to view how life for many people might have transpired if he had never been born and his life had never intersected with theirs. He was able to understand what would be impossible for any of us to know: how his words and actions, even his simple presence, had rippled out and affected the courses of so many other lives. With this perspective, he decided not to end his life by drowning as he had planned. The insight he was able to uncover during his experience ultimately helped him to decide not only to *live*, but to *live well*.

I feel as if I've been given a similar opportunity, through working with the dying and seeing firsthand the fragility and impermanence of the thread of life. Although I struggle, like every other human being, with the daily challenges of overwork, impatience, fear, anger, and disappointment, I know that it is always *my choice* instead to choose happiness, forgiveness, compassion, and joy, to live each day as if it were my last, and to be grateful for every day that I have.

Working with the dying has brought light into my own life, illuminating the shadowy corners of negativity that I alone have the choice to relinquish or to transform to something more positive. Even though the work I do is with the dying, it has also been work within *myself*, and I thank God every day for both of those opportunities.

So, in the end, what is it that the dying teach others around them? They teach how to love and how to allow ourselves to be loved; how to forgive and how to ask for forgiveness; how to find our joy and how to spread that joy around to others. They also teach us how to spend valuable time connecting our earthly self with our spiritual self so that these two separate but vital aspects of our being aren't strangers when they meet as the time of our own death draws near.

And so it is perhaps meant to be that, with every person's dying, another person is learning to *live well.*

Although I can't know for certain, I suspect from what I have witnessed that, possibly, the very best part of living might actually be the dying.

To live in the hearts of those we leave behind is not to die.
—Joseph Campbell

Index

Quest Books

encourages open-minded inquiry into world religions, philosophy, science, and the arts in order to understand the wisdom of the ages, respect the unity of all life, and help people explore individual spiritual self-transformation.

Its publications are generously supported by The Kern Foundation, a trust committed to Theosophical education.

Quest Books is the imprint of the Theosophical Publishing House, a division of the Theosophical Society in America. For information about programs, literature, on-line study, membership benefits, and international centers, see www.theosophical.org or call 800-669-1571 or (outside the U.S.) 630-668-1571.

Related Quest Titles

Death at the Movies: Hollywood's Guide to the Hereafter, by Lyn and Tom Davis Genelli

In Times of Grief, by Connie Harrison

Letters to a Dying Friend, by Anton Grosz